TEST YOUR
INTELLIGENCE

BRAIN
BUSTERS

PHILIP J. CARTER &
KEN A. RUSSELL

JOINT EDITORS OF THE MENSA UK PUZZLE GROUP JOURNAL

WARD LOCK

A WARD LOCK BOOK

First published in the UK 1992
by Ward Lock
(a Cassell imprint)
Villiers House
41/47 Strand
LONDON
WC2N 5JE

Distributed in the United States
by Sterling Publishing Co., Inc.
387 Park Avenue South, New York, NY 10016–8810

Distributed in Australia
by Capricorn Link (Australia) Pty Ltd
P.O. Box 665, Lane Cove, NSW 2066

British Library Cataloguing-in-Publication Data.
A catalogue record for this book is available from the British Library

ISBN 0 7063 7097 X

Typeset in Great Britain

Printed and bound in Great Britain
by Cox and Wyman Ltd.

BRAIN
BUSTERS

CONTENTS

Acknowledgements 6
Introduction 7

About the Puzzles 8
Sequences and
    Relationships 9
Themes 20
Odd One Out (i) 31
Anagrams 35
Numbers 43
Categorise 54
Rebuses 59
Quotations (i) 64
Brainbenders 69
Missing Links 76
Teasers 85
Words (i) 92
Codes 100
Beyond Your Ken? 104

Mental Exercises 111
Puzzles of the Mind 116
Gambling and Probability 122
Crosswords 126
Cryptograms 134
Kickself (i) 139

Anagrams Galore 147
Numbers in Wonderland 155
Odd One Out (ii) 161
Words (ii) 166
The World of Numbers 174
Quotations (ii) 180
Brainbenders for
    Mentalathletes 185
Wind-ups 191

Potpourri 198
More Anagrams 205
More Numbers 214
Word Play 224
Diagrams 237
Quotations (iii) 243
Magic Squares 248
Kickself (ii) 257
Codes and Ciphers 264
Crossword Variations 269
More Brainbenders 283
Russell Squares 291
Et Cetera 295

Answers 305

ACKNOWLEDGEMENTS

We wish to thank the British Mensa Committee and the Mensa Executive Director, Harold Gale, for their continued support for all our projects. Special thanks are due to all members of Enigmasig for their support, interest and lively correspondence. A huge amount of thanks go to our wives, both named Barbara, for their enthusiasm, optimism and invaluable assistance with checking puzzles and preparing typescripts; without their support this book would not have been possible.

(Publisher's Note: all references to Mensa relate to British Mensa Ltd)

INTRODUCTION

We are delighted to have had the opportunity to produce this book and to be able to share our interest in puzzles with you. It is through our membership of Mensa, the High-IQ society, and in particular our involvement with Enigmasig, the special-interest group within Mensa devoted to the setting and solving of puzzles, that the two of us have formed the friendship and partnership which has led to a series of books and has enabled us continually to devise new and original types of puzzles.

Founded in 1946, Mensa is a society where the sole qualification for membership is to have attained a score, in any supervised test of general intelligence, which puts the applicant in the top 2 per cent of the general population. The name 'Mensa' is Latin for 'table', indicating a round table society which aims to include intelligent people of every opinion and calling, where all members are of equal standing within the society.

Mensa is perhaps best described as a social club where members communicate with other members through correspondence, meetings, think-ins, dinners, special-interest groups, magazines, lectures and international gatherings. Membership of the society gives us enormous interest and pleasure. If you wish to learn more about Mensa, and how to take the Mensa Entrance Test, then why not write for details to one of the addresses below? If you are successful, then we are sure you will find that the efforts involved are far outweighed by the enjoyment you will derive.

UK
British Mensa Ltd
Mensa House
St John's Square
Wolverhampton
WV2 4AH

USA
American Mensa Ltd
2626 E14 Street
Brooklyn
NY 11235

Australia
Australian Mensa Incorporated
PO Box 213
Toonak
Victoria 3142

International
Mensa International Ltd
15 The Ivories
6–8 Northampton Street
London N1 2HY

ABOUT THE PUZZLES

To enable you to monitor your performance throughout the book
we have allocated to each puzzle one of the following star ratings;

* Standard
** More challenging
*** Difficult
**** Appallingly difficult

THE ANSWERS

The answers to all the questions are at the end of the book on
pages 305–364, and are numbered 1–382.

Please note that the answers to the questions are *not* in numerical
order so that there is no risk of seeing the answer to the next
puzzle before you have tackled it. The number of the answer you
need is in brackets next to each question.

SEQUENCES AND RELATIONSHIPS

Sequences have been chosen for the first group of puzzles, as they are a great way of sharpening up the mind. With one exception, no specific general knowledge is required, but what is necessary is to analyse and identify logical patterns or relationships between words, numbers or diagrams and decide what should follow, either to continue or to complete the sequence, or alternatively decide what, more appropriately, will match the given list.

In the grids, sequences of numbers, which would be familiar if written out conventionally, are made much trickier by converting them into number mazes.

Find the Sequence

There is a logical way to get from the top left-hand square to the bottom right by moving from square to square horizontally, vertically or diagonally and visiting every square once only. What is it?

START

3	6	5	3	5	9
7	9	1	6	8	0
2	8	1	6	4	9
1	7	8	9	7	1
2	2	4	1	1	7
9	7	3	2	4	7

FINISH

(See A34)

Find the pair to complete the following sequence.

Choose from:

    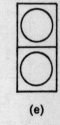

(a)   (b)   (c)   (d)   (e)

(See A47)

3
Find the Next Number

In each of the following, find the number which should logically come next in sequence:

  *(a)   266,   196,   256,   169,   ?

**(b)   126,   72,   648,   512,   9216,   1472,   ?

***(c) Consider the number 864. Now complete the following sequence:

       52,   54,   72,   76,   94,   ?

(See A64)

Travel out of the number maze by finding a meaningful route, starting at the middle square and moving to the top right from square to square horizontally, vertically or diagonally and visiting every square once only.

1	1	5	1	3	**OUT**
1	7	3	4	4	
3	2	*	3	7	
1	1	2	2	3	
7	9	9	3	1	

(See A11)

*(a)   Find the next letter in this sequence:

TFSETTFSETTTT

***(b)   Find the next most suitable letter:

A, H, I, M

Choose from:

N, P, Q, R, T, V, X

***(c)   Find the next most suitable letter:

F, G, J, L

Choose from:

N, P, S, V, W, Y

(See A23)

Words

In each of the following choose a word which you think will best
match the rest.

**(a) AGE, DATE, KIND, FULLY, POWER

Choose one from:

RAP, STRUT, BULLY, HOOD, CRIME,
YEAR

**(b) HINT, DIRT, COSY, FORT

Choose one from:

KNOT, PART, EPIC, ROUT, NAVY

*(c) MANOEUVRING, CAULIFLOWER,
ACCENTUATION, BEHAVIOURISM,
GREGARIOUS

Choose one from:

MANUSCRIPT, CAUTIONED,
MATRICULATION, OBSTREPEROUS,
REORIENTATION

(See A15)

Find the next most appropriate square.

Choose from:

   (a)   (b)   (c)   (d)   (e)   (f)

(See A25)

Find the next drawing.

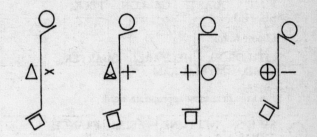

Choose from:

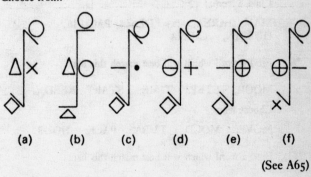

  (a)   (b)   (c)   (d)   (e)   (f)

(See A65)

*(a)   Find the next in sequence:

PINT,   QUART,   GALLON,   PECK,
BUSHEL,   ?

Choose from:

CHALDRON,   HECTARE,   QUARTER,
LOAD,   MYRIAGRAM

**(b)   Find the next most appropriate word:

SIRIUS,   NEPTUNE,   ASIA,   FRANCE,
TEXAS,   ?

Choose from:

MAN,   AREA,   SWEDEN,   PACIFIC,
DUBLIN,   CHINA

*(c)   Find a word which will best match this list:

MOOR,   STEP,   TIME,   STAR,   REED,

Choose from:

MOVE,   MOLD,   TUBA,   PACE,   HOUR

**(d)   Find a word which will best match this list:

VICE,   BODY,   TABIE,   WHERE,   ?

Choose from:

CHAIR,   ARM,   HEAD,   MAD,   LEER

(See A49)

Find the next circle.

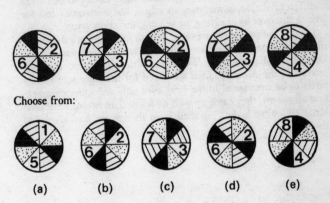

Choose from:

(a)　　　(b)　　　(c)　　　(d)　　　(e)

(See A56)

THEMES

As a contrast to the previous chapter good general knowledge is the main requirement here rather than logic. Each puzzle covers a different theme, sometimes specified, but sometimes left for you to discover by studying, or solving, the clues given.

One of the puzzles proves that Mensa members are dedicated puzzle solvers and will even provide answers which you did not know existed. When the 'Feathered Friends' puzzle (15) appeared in the *Mensa* Journal we asked for the names of twenty birds to be uncovered in the grid. Not only did some members find all twenty, they came up with no fewer than twelve additional birds which we hadn't spotted even though we had compiled the puzzle!

Fill in the composers below. The marked letters are an anagram of one of the composers' works.

1. – A – H – A – I – ☐ – O – ☐

2. ☐ – O – N – D

3. – C – U – A – N

4. – E – T – O – E – ☐

5. – L – A –

6. – I – E – ☐

7. – S – H – ☐ – I – O – S – Y

8. ☐ – A – ☐ – C – G – I

9. – C – U – E – T

10. – E – D – L – S – ☐ – H –

11. – E – E – B – E – ☐

12. – E – L – ☐ – O –

13. – U – C – N –

14. – T – A – ☐ – S – Y

15. – A – N – ☐ – R

(See A41)

(All in chronological order.)

THE T.W.

D. OF A. THE G. AT B.

R. I. OF B.

R. OF B.

THE D. A.

THE N.C. OF E.

M.C.S. BY K.J

THE M.P.

THE H.Y.W.

THE R. OF W.T.

THE B. OF A.

J. OF A. B. AT R.

W. OF THE R.E. BY B. OF B.

C.C.D.A.

S.F.D.S.R.W.

THE G.P.

C.W. IN E.

O.C.B.L.P.

G.F. OF L.

A. OF P. THE G. OF R.

U. OF E. AND S.

THE S.S.B.

(See A24)

Fill in the countries below. The first letter of each country is an anagram of another country and its capital.

1. – N – I – U –
2. – A – T – N – Q – E
3. – E – C – E – L – S
4. – U – A –
5. – G – N – A
6. – E – E –
7. – U – A –
8. – L – E – I –
9. – N – O – A
10. – N – O – E – I –
11. – E – E – A –
12. – O – O – B – A
13. – W – N – A

(See A16)

Oxymorons

What is an oxymoron? The answer is a very rarely used word describing a very often used figure of speech in which two words of opposite meaning are linked together to form a descriptive phrase, e.g. golfers play with metal woods and make good bad shots, and snooker players sometimes thin the ball too thickly.

The following is our compilation of oxymorons. Column two has been mixed up and should be paired with a word in column one.

1.	Fine	History
2.	Dry	Permanent Secretary
3.	Awfully	Jump
4.	Slipped	The rear
5.	Sweet	Chilli
6.	Good	Games
7.	Stand	Sherry
8.	Standing	Good
9.	Retired	Goods
10.	Future	Grief
11.	Sit	Fit
12.	War	Beginners
13.	Spend	Sweet
14.	Perfectly	Drizzle
15.	Advance to	Numb
16.	Advanced	Thrift
17.	Feeling	Awful
18.	Bitter	Down
19.	Loose	Up
20.	Hot	Sorrow
21.	Bad	Up

(See A80)

By moving from square to square horizontally, vertically or diagonally it is possible to find the names of 32 birds in the grid below. Squares may be used more than once but not in the same name. There are no redundant squares.

N	I	O	L	N	I	W	I
I	O	R	C	E	D	R	N
B	K	U	E	G	R	T	G
O	C	T	N	W	A	R	O
R	R	J	N	I	P	K	W
O	M	A	L	A	R	S	A
E	Y	G	L	D	O	E	N
I	P	A	R	V	E	V	E

(See A70)

Complete the Grid

First find the theme, then fill in the names.

1. A – – M –
2. E – – – – – – – – –
3. – – R –
4. – I – – – – – –
5. – – C – – – A –
6. N – – – –
7. P – – – – –
8. – – – – R – – –
9. – E – – – –
10. – – – – S
11. – I – – – –
12. – – – – – – – – D
13. – – – – E –
14. – – – N –
15. T – – – –
16. – – S – – –

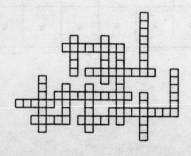

(See A40)

(All in chronological order.)

THE B. OF P.P.

THE B.H. OF C.

C. OF Q. BY W.

S.J.I. BY J.H.

A.W. OF I.

G.W.B.F.P. OF U.S.

O. OF THE F.R.

B. OF THE N.

N.B.B.E. OF F.

I. OF R. BY N.

B. OF W.

THE C.W.

THE A.C.W.

P. OF Q.V. AS E. OF I.

T.I. BY A.G.B.

R.V. OF N.T.P.

B. OF THE B.W.

(See A57)

Moving from square to square horizontally, vertically or diagonally find 24 words connected with an orchestra in the grid below. Squares may be used more than once but not in the same name. There are no redundant squares.

O	L	A	S	O	F	U	T	R	U
L	B	R	N	S	O	L	O	E	M
E	C	O	C	D	L	N	C	T	P
C	H	I	E	U	A	H	C	R	U
G	N	R	C	B	R	I	I	B	E
S	S	T	Y	M	W	P	A	S	L
I	O	U	C	P	O	A	N	M	L
N	M	R	E	D	O	L	G	U	B
O	B	G	T	I	W	I	E	R	G
N	E	A	N	D	V	N	D	E	L

(See A26)

(a)   *E PLURIBUS UNUM*

Fill in the blanks. The first letter of each spells out
another in the same theme.

1.   – I – N – S – T –
2.   – – – A – O – A
3.   – E – R – S – –
4.   – E – – E – – – E
5.   – – – A – S – S
6.   – E –   – E – – E –   (2 words)
7.   – – A – A – A

*(b)   Fill in the words. The marked letters form an anagram
which explains the puzzle.

0.   ⊟ A – M
1.   – I – H –   – I |R| (2 words)
2.   ⊟ – – G – T   – R – E – E   (2 words)
3.   – E – T ⊟ E   – R – E – E   (2 words)
4.   – O – E – A – E   – R – E – |E| (2 words)
5.   ⊟ R – S –   ⊟ R – E – E   (2 words)
6.   – T – O – –   – R – E – E   (2 words)
7.   – O – E – A ⊟ E   – |A| – E   (2 words)
8.   – R – S –   – A – E   (2 words)
9.   – T – |O| – G   – A – E   (2 words)
10. – H – L –   – A – |E| (2 words)
11. – T – R –
12. – ⊟ – R – C ⊟ N –

(See A32)

Three Cs

The following is a list of countries with their capitals and currency;
however they have all been mixed up. Try to match them up again.

COUNTRY	CAPITAL	CURRENCY
Gambia	Male	Lek
Mongolia	Conakry	Colon
Guinea	Hamilton	Kip
Honduras	Doha	Franc
Costa Rica	Khartoum	Syli
Gabon	Tirana	Rupee
Laos	San Jose	Escudo
Paraguay	Ulan Bator	Pound
Albania	Vientiane	Riyal
Azores	Banjul	Guarani
Bermuda	Asuncion	Tughrik
Qatar	Tegucigalpa	Dollar
Maldive Islands	Libreville	Dalasi
Sudan	Ponta Delgada	Lampira

(See A6)

Remember, do not always look for the obvious—things are not always what they appear to be.

***(a)   Which is the odd one out?

    1. Chain

    2. Mail

    3. Plane

    4. Train

    5. Reign

    6. Rain

*(b)   Which is the odd one out?

    1. Credit

    2. Energy

    3. Asleep

    4. Range

    5. Leased

    6. Greeny

    7. Tender

    8. Please

    9. Direct

    10. Anger

    11. Rented

(See A66)

(a) Which of the following numbers is different to the rest?

1. 743218
2. 781138
3. 786116
4. 764124
5. 781234

(b) Find the odd one out.

7924, 4682, 3973, 3199, 2785

(See A19)

One of the following pairs does not belong with the others. Which is it?

1. Mike and Victor

2. Romeo and Juliet

3. Quebec and Lima

4. Rum and Brandy

5. Tango and Foxtrot

(See A33)

ANAGRAMS

There are a total of 41 anagrams which should satisfy the appetites of most anagram enthusiasts. The wheels have the added challenge of finding words from the anagram clues and the 'Enigmasig Wheels' are named after the Special Interest Group within Mensa mentioned in the introduction. Apart from the wheels, the anagrams are presented in a way which will become clear as you begin to solve them.

Complete the word in each column (all end in 'E'). Clues are anagrams in section to right of each column.

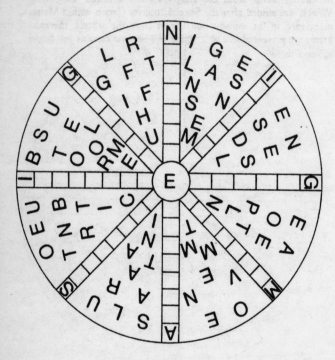

(See A51)

The Enigmasig Wheel (Mark II)

The anagrams in each section are a clue to both the word in the column to the left of each section (all end in 'E') and the word above the section (beginning and ending with the initial letters in the adjoining columns and reading clockwise).

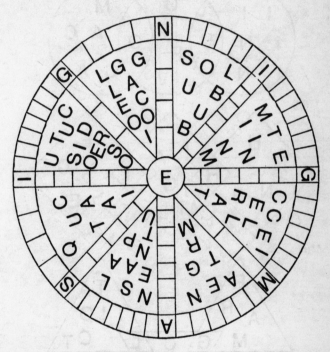

(See A77)

Solve the anagrams below. There are no two adjoining letters in the same circle/square/triangle.

*(a)

**(b)

**(c)

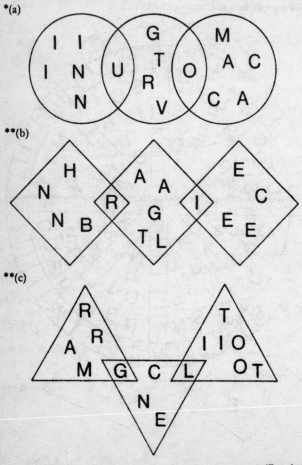

(See A7)

Anagrams

Solve the anagrams below. There are no two adjoining letters in the same shape.

**(a)

**(b)

*(c)

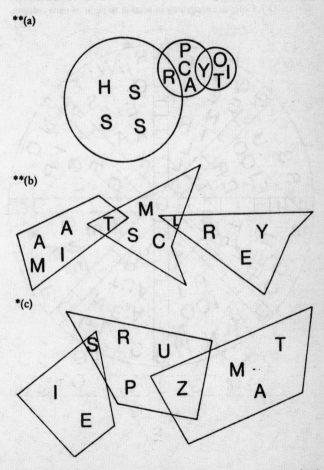

(See A50)

The name given to this puzzle is the old fairground name for the roundabout ride on horses. Complete the words in each column (all end in 'G'). Clues are anagrams in section to right of each column.

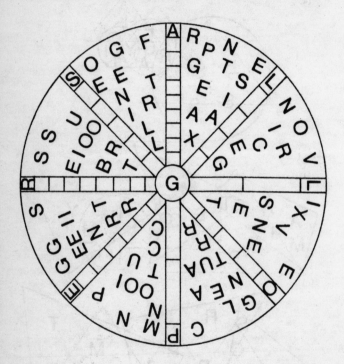

(See A81)

Solve the anagrams below. There are no two adjoining letters in the same shape.

**(a)

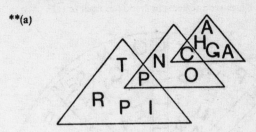

**(b)

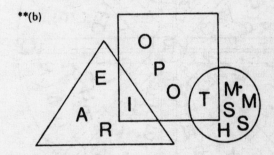

**(c)

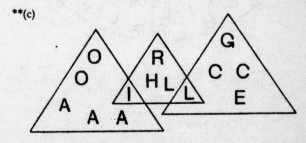

(See A90)

Complete the word in each column (all end in 'R'). Clues are anagrams in section to right of each column.

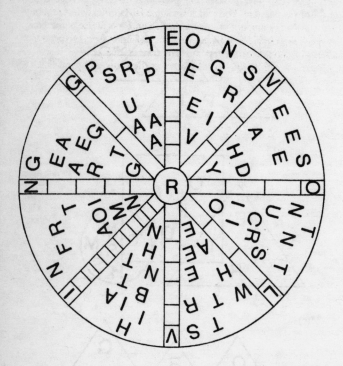

(See A10)

NUMBERS

Numbers can be interesting and challenging but often confusing, and it is fascinating how some numbers have their own individual characteristics. The puzzles are presented to give as varied a challenge as possible. You will solve some fairly quickly but others may need a fair amount of juggling with numbers. Please persevere as you will probably gain a great deal of satisfaction from sorting out a mass of digits to arrive finally at the correct answer.

Numbers can be fun, so calculators at the ready and good luck!

In each of the following place the digits into the grid so that each horizontal and vertical line can be divided by 11 reading either forwards or backwards.

(a) 2, 2, 3, 3,
4, 4, 4, 4,
6, 6, 6,
7, 7, 7, 7, 8

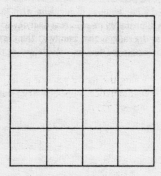

(b) 1, 1, 1, 2, 2,
3, 3, 3, 3,
4, 4, 6,
8, 9, 9, 9

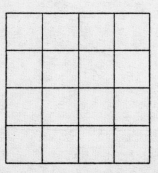

(If you find yourself struggling you may find it helpful to refer to puzzle 96 (a).)

(See A67)

Find the Calculation

***(a) Using the figure 5 eight times together with any mathematical symbols, with the exception of plus signs, write out a calculation to give the answer 110. Find two answers.

**(b) Using the figure 6 seven times, together with any mathematical symbols, write out a calculation to give the answer 5832.

*(c) Using the figure 7 seven times, together with any mathematical symbols, write out a calculation to give the answer 7777.

(See A2)

Place all the digits below in the grid so that all the numbers when read both forwards and backwards are divisible by 37. Lines reading downwards contain the following numbers:

(A) 1, 1, 1, 1, 1, 1, 3

(B) 2, 3, 4, 4, 5, 5, 6, 8, 9

(C) 3, 3, 5, 7, 8, 9

(D) 1, 1, 2, 2, 2, 7, 8, 8, 8

(E) 1, 5

(F) 1, 2, 2, 7, 7, 8

(G) 1, 1, 6, 7, 7, 7

(H) 4, 5, 6, 6, 7, 8

(I) 2, 2, 2, 3, 3, 3, 5, 6, 7, 9

(J) 2, 2, 5, 5, 6, 9

(K) 0, 2, 2, 3, 3, 6, 6, 7

(L) 2, 2, 2, 4, 4, 6

(See A42)

I won all three major knockout competitions at my Golf Club last year (wishful thinking) even though I was the only player unlucky enough to be drawn in both preliminary rounds.

Recently our club statistician stopped me and said, 'Do you know, I cubed the number of entrants for each competition and the last digit of each of the three resultant numbers is the same as your golf handicap and the sum of the three middle digits, i.e. the middle digit of each of the three cube numbers, is the same as mine; also the total number of rounds you won is the same as your wife's handicap which is exactly double your own handicap; furthermore the total number of matches played, including the end of season consolation event for players knocked out in the preliminary rounds, is the same as the age of Seth Arkwright, our oldest surviving founder member?'

What are mine, my wife's and the club statistician's handicaps and how old is Seth Arkwright?

(See A14)

The Magic Number Nine

Place the digits below into the grid in such a way that all the horizontal and vertical lines when read both forwards and backwards will divide exactly by 9. It will assist you in knowing that the sum of the digits of each line will also divide by nine.

1, 1, 1, 2, 2, 2, 2, 2, 3, 3, 4, 4, 4, 5, 5, 6, 7, 7, 7, 7, 8, 8, 8, 9, 9.

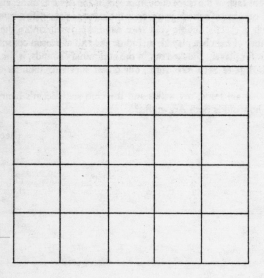

(See A13)

Missing Numbers

In each of the following find the missing numbers:

*(a)   2, 3, 4, 6, 8, 12, ?, ?, 32, 48, 96.

*(b)   1, 5, 14, 30, 55, ?, 140.

*(c)   2, 3, 4, 6, 9, 12, ?, 36.

(See A69)

Place the digits in the track in such a way that the sum of any three consecutive digits round the track can be divided by three.

1, 1, 1, 1, 2, 2, 2, 3, 3, 3, 3, 4, 4, 5, 5, 5, 5, 5, 6, 6, 6, 6, 7, 7, 7, 7, 8, 8, 9, 9, 9.

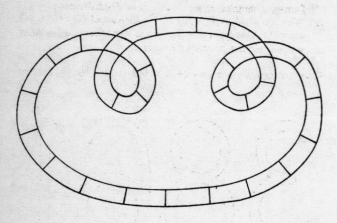

(See A52)

Two workmen were putting the finishing touches to a new door they had fitted to house number 3861. All that was left to do was screw the metal digits to the door.

(a) Being a Mensan, Phil could not resist challenging Ken by asking him if he could screw the digits onto the door to give a four figure number which could not be divided exactly by 9.

(b) When they had sorted that out Ken then asked Phil if he could screw the same digits onto the door to give a four figure number which could not be divided exactly by 3.

What is the answer to both problems? Can either of them be done?

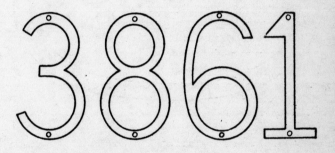

(See A59)

*(a) Fill in the digits from 1 to 9 to complete the addition sum.

$$
\begin{array}{cccc}
 & * & * & * \\
 & * & * & * \\
 & * & * & * \\
\hline
1 & 9 & 0 & 8 \\
\end{array}
$$

***(b) By using the digits 0–9 once each only (excluding the answer) devise an addition sum to give the answer 52.2.

(See A9)

Cubes and Squares

This puzzle almost made the Brainbender section. If you haven't a calculator we hope you have plenty of fingers and toes.

ACROSS

- A. CUBE
- E. SQUARE
- G. CUBE
- H. SQUARE
- I. SQUARE
- L. SQUARE
- M. CUBE
- P. CUBE
- Q. CUBE
- R. SQUARE

DOWN

- A. CUBE
- B. CUBE
- C. SQUARE
- D. CUBE
- E. CUBE
- F. CUBE/SQUARE
- J. CUBE
- K. CUBE
- L. SQUARE
- N. SQUARE
- O. SQUARE

(See A78)

CATEGORISE

The word puzzles in this chapter are the second of the general knowledge sections in the book. Dividing the groups into threes will not prove as easy as it appears at first glance but this should make it all the more interesting.

Arrange into groups of three

Abode
Bar
Bicycle
Home
Lever
Macmillan
Pedal
Residence
Rod
Roof
Straw
Thatcher

(See A36)

**42
Arrange into groups of three

Argon
Chamois
Corsica
Crete
Cyprus
Eland
Elba
Gallium
Sardinia
St Helena
Xenon
Zebu

(See A58)

***43
Arrange into groups of three

121
148
157
162
174
246
277
389
437
575
633
681

(See A68)

Ashdod
Creation
Elijah
Haydn
Hebrides
Israel
Jaffa
Mendelssohn
Minch
Seasons
Stornoway
Western Isles

(See A27)

Arrange into groups of three

Brobdingnag
Excursion
Expedition
Fast
Journey
Lilliput
Migration
Quick
Rapid
Swallow
Swift
Travels

(See A20)

Arrange into groups of three

Agamemnon
Congo
Copenhagen
Elias
Helsinki
Kamet
Kenya
Niger
Nile
Obi
Oslo
Stockholm

(See A53)

REBUSES

Not everyone will be familiar with the word 'rebus', however, most people will recall books at school where the words were represented by pictures and symbols. Well these are rebuses.

To give a couple of examples:

might represent 'TEA-TIME' and

```
        o
        o
AYE     o
        o
        o
```

might represent 'HAWAII 50'

You really will need to use your imagination to solve the rebuses that follow and then you will probably wish to have a go at inventing some of your own.

Solve the Rebus

```
        T
     T     T
  T     T     T
T   T     T   T
```

(See A21)

Solve the Rebus

```
      N N
    N     N
  N         N
 N           N
  N         N
   N       N
    N     N
     N N
```

(See A88)

Solve the Rebus

```
| | | | | | | | | |
SSSSSSSSSS
```

(See A37)

Solve the Rebus

(See A62)

Solve the Rebus

```
::
::
::
::::::
```

(See A98)

Solve the Rebus

```
                    l
       i i i i i i
```

(See A39)

DES
DES

(See A71)

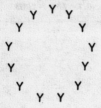

(See A96)

Solve the Rebus

YAW

(See A44)

Solve the Rebus

N
W
O
D

(See A87)

QUOTATIONS (i)

Eight quotations are to be found in this section in a variety of disguises. Great enjoyment can be obtained from reading quotations and it is often surprising to find who originated, hundreds, sometimes thousands, of years ago, phrases we still use frequently today in our every day speech. The following, for example, were all written by the same man:

'The world's mine oyster'
'The better part of valour is discretion'
'Be to yourself as you would to your friend'
'If money go before all ways do lie open'
'All that glisters is not gold'
'Ill blows the wind that profits nobody'

An anagram of his name is, very aptly, 'I'll make a wise phrase'.

(See A43)

In each of the following, two quotations are squashed together. All
the letters are in the correct order. Find the two quotations. To
assist, the writers' names follow the quotations but have been put
together in the same way.

**(a) FALORLTGHEINTFORGSGCIOVMEETCOOHNIC
MLUWHDOWEAINLDLBBUEAGTW⁄RAIETED.
    — SLOHNGAFKELESLPOEAWRE

**(b) TAHEBSONENLCEYMWAAYKETSTOHEHHAEAV
REATFGRRIOEWNFDONISDTEOBREONE.
    — EMBEARYSLOYN

(See A84)

Starting at the top left-hand corner, work horizontally, vertically and diagonally to find some useful philosophy. Nine letters are redundant which form an anagram of the philosopher who wrote this (a long time ago).

START

T	S	P	N	T	E	D	U
I	H	I	H	N	T	E	S
E	E	W	E	T	U	H	P
T	R	R	O	R	E	A	P
O	S	R	O	B	A	H	Y
C	F	F	E	E	R	C	E
H	T	S	C	S	O	H	G
I	A	N	E	F	A	N	I

(See A91)

In each of the following find the starting point, fill in the blanks and a quotation will appear. The missing letters form an anagram of the writer.

*(a)

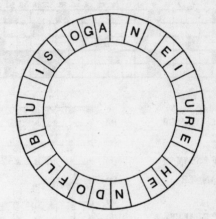

**(b)

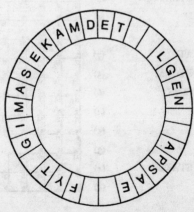

(See A100)

Solve the clues, place each letter in its appropriate position in the grid and a quotation will appear.

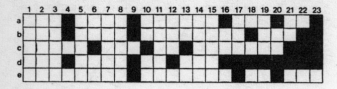

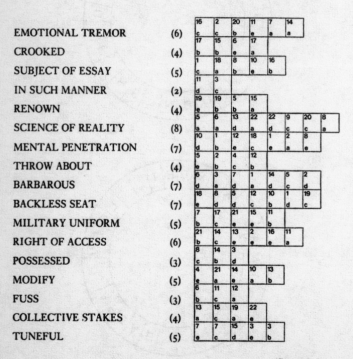

EMOTIONAL TREMOR	(6)
CROOKED	(4)
SUBJECT OF ESSAY	(5)
IN SUCH MANNER	(2)
RENOWN	(4)
SCIENCE OF REALITY	(8)
MENTAL PENETRATION	(7)
THROW ABOUT	(4)
BARBAROUS	(7)
BACKLESS SEAT	(7)
MILITARY UNIFORM	(5)
RIGHT OF ACCESS	(6)
POSSESSED	(3)
MODIFY	(5)
FUSS	(3)
COLLECTIVE STAKES	(4)
TUNEFUL	(5)

(See A85)

BRAINBENDERS

This section is named 'Brainbenders' simply because we believe the puzzles to be some of the most difficult in the book. If we had to choose the most difficult of them all it would be the cross-alphabet (64), but remember every puzzle has a solution and can be solved, eventually.

The explorer goes through the maze to the treasure chest by moving from letter to letter, vertically, horizontally or diagonally to discover the hidden message. There are seven redundant letters which are an anagram of the contents of the treasure chest.

ENTER

Y	W	A	F	O	O	N	O
U	O	E	R	F	R	C	N
R	R	D	S	E	T	D	G
F	S	G	I	A	N	R	T
R	O	H	R	E	A	U	A
T	T	S	T	S	N	A	L
A	F	I	A	O	T	I	O
N	C	T	I	H	I	N	S

TREASURE CHEST

(See A97)

70

Squares

Complete the grid below to give square numbers only using the following digits (2 already filled in):

1, 1, 1, 1, 1, 2, 2, 2, 2, 2, 2, 2, 2, (3), 4, 4, 4, 4, 4, 4,
5, 5, 5, 5, (6), 6, 6, 6, 6, 6, 7, 8, 8, 8, 8, 9, 9, 9, 9, 9, 0.

(See A95)

Fill in the missing letters.

D	I	G	I
I	O	N	
	I		A
S	E	R	P

(See A8)

This is the first of several cross-alphabet puzzles we have included in this book. This one is included in the Brainbender section because it is the most difficult. Some months ago a similar puzzle appeared in the *Mensa* Journal and was solved by only one person, so if you are successful you know just how well you have done. The object is to put each of the 26 letters of the alphabet into the grid once only to form a crossword. There are no clues; what is required is a great deal of juggling with letters and words.

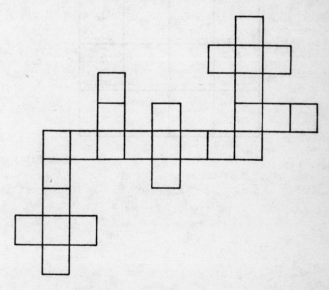

(See A99)

A Magic Number Square

Fill the grid below with the numbers 1–16 to form a magic square so that each vertical and horizontal line, each corner to corner diagonal line, the four corner numbers, each block of four corner squares and the middle four block of numbers each add up to 34. Number 7 filled in for good luck.

7			

(See A101)

Ego Booster

Commence at the top left-hand corner and travel to the bottom right-hand corner by moving from letter to letter, vertically, horizontally or diagonally to unscramble the hidden message. Visit each square once only. There are no redundant letters.

START

W	E	S	I	H	B	E	Y	D	D
C	H	S	F	S	T	D	O	N	O
C	U	E	P	U	E	E	T	B	U
S	N	L	L	U	V	T	I	Q	A
U	Y	Y	Z	O	E	T	I	L	U
C	O	Z	R	L	S	E	N	A	N
Y	O	L	P	P	O	I	O	P	D
O	E	M	E	F	A	T	A	T	I
W	U	L	V	D	N	I	R	N	E
I	L	H	A	E	T	E	M	C	E

FINISH

(See A72)

MISSING LINKS

This is very similar to the first section in that you are required to identify relationships between numbers, words and diagrammatic representation. You will need to open your mind to every possibility, be prepared for the unexpected and not take everything at face value. Then you will start coming up with the right answers.

**67
Fill in the Missing Numbers

74862	2688	

82687		630

79988		

(See A82)

**68
Fill in the Missing Numbers

15707	3.1.44	

	6·10·47	19444

26632		

(See A28)

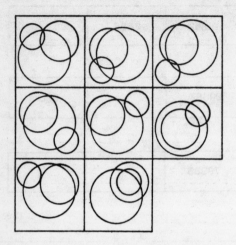

Choose from:

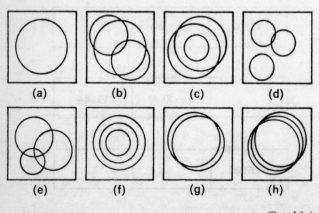

(a)   (b)   (c)   (d)

(e)   (f)   (g)   (h)

(See A60)

Fill in the Missing Numbers

1248		4096

428		

4812	8	

(See A1)

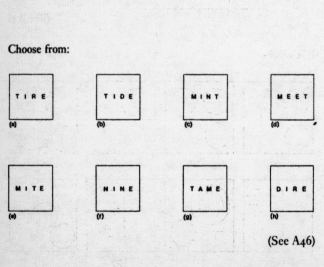

E - I -	- M - -	T - - -
T - - -	R - - E	- M I -
D - - -	- I - -	?

Choose from:

| (a) TIRE | (b) TIDE | (c) MINT | (d) MEET |
| (e) MITE | (f) NINE | (g) TAME | (h) DIRE |

(See A46)

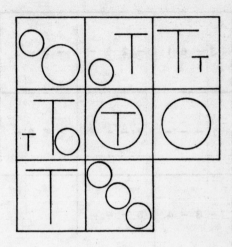

Choose from:

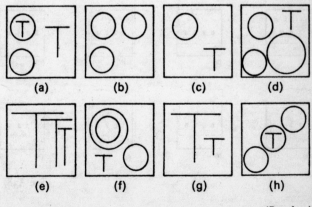

(a) (b) (c) (d)

(e) (f) (g) (h)

(See A55)

Fill in the Missing Numbers
then Find the Missing Square

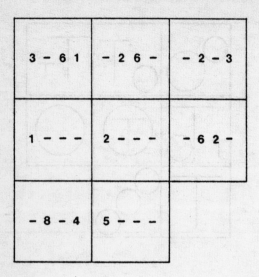

3 – 6 1	– 2 6 –	– 2 – 3
1 – – –	2 – – –	– 6 2 –
– 8 – 4	5 – – –	

Choose from:

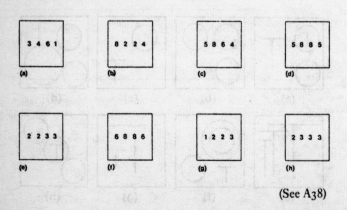

3 4 6 1	8 2 2 4	5 8 6 4	5 8 8 5
(a)	(b)	(c)	(d)

2 2 3 3	6 8 8 6	1 2 2 3	2 3 3 3
(e)	(f)	(g)	(h)

(See A38)

3		6	30

9	15	20	180

8	9	15	16	20	

(See A29)

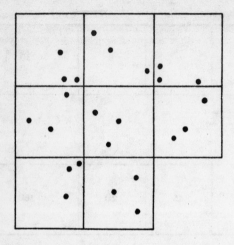

Choose from:

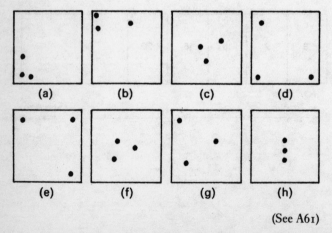

(See A61)

A selection of eight teasers. You will probably spot the answers to some fairly quickly but others just may trick you and it will be those that you will wish to try out on your friends.

There was a total of 229 matches played in our local open amateur knockout Tiddlywinks Championships last year. One player scratched out of the preliminary round because of illness and another from the third round because of holidays. Without doing any written calculation can you say how many players entered the competition?

(See A73)

Spin the Wheel

If a wheel is spun containing an equal number of black and white segments, what are the chances of each of the following combinations appearing against an arrow above the top of the wheel in any two consecutive spins?

        (a)   White—white
        (b)   White—black

(See A12)

When I was a schoolboy I composed and memorised the following. For what purpose?

'Now I know a super utterance to assist maths.'

(See A22)

Town Hall Clock

On the evening before the night when the clocks were put back an hour to mark the end of Summer Time Mr Riddle phoned his solicitor to makē an appointment for the following morning. When the solicitor asked the time of the appointment Mr Riddle said '11 hours after it takes the Town Hall clock 10 seconds to strike the hour.' 'Doesn't the Town Hall clock strike at 1-second intervals?', asked the solicitor. 'Yes,' said Mr Riddle. 'OK, then, that's easy enough to work out,' said the solicitor. What was the time of the appointment?

(See A45)

*80
Colours

How many colours are necessary to fill in the grid below so that no two sections containing the same colours have adjoining boundaries.

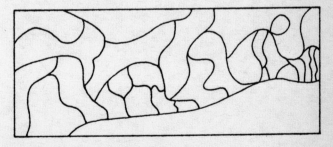

(See A3)

Cardboard Boxes

A cardboard box manufacturer was considering doubling the volume of his square boxes. On hearing of this his supplier of cardboard decided to encourage him to place the extra business by offering a very generous 37.5 per cent quantity discount on his new total turnover figure. How much extra would the box manufacturer have to pay for the additional cardboard if he decided to go ahead?

(See A54)

Wooden Cubes

By using two wooden cubes placed side by side and by numbering each side of each cube with one digit only, what is the highest number which can be displayed by starting at 1 then working upwards and not omitting any subsequent numbers?

Both cubes must be used for each number but they can be switched round.

(See A17)

The Generous Duke

The kindly Duke decided to give three of his servants a piece of land each as a long service award. He gave each a length of wire 144 yards long and some posts and instructed the first to mark out his land in the form of an equilateral triangle, the second in the form of a circle and the third in the form of a square. Which, if any, received the greatest area of land and which received least?

(See A48)

60 words to be found in various disguises. The type of puzzle, like anagrams, that looks easy once you know the answer. Personally, we find the Cross-Alphabet puzzles fascinating to compile and always try to achieve as compact a version as possible. We would be interested to learn which is the most compact X-Alpha puzzle possible in the English language. The ultimate 'impossible' version would be to insert the 26 letters of the alphabet into the grid below so that each horizontal and vertical line forms a word.

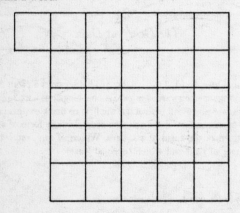

We very much doubt, however, if it would be possible to get near to this as only five vowels would kill any attempt. Probably the only way to find the most compact version would be with the aid of a computer and a data base consisting of all the words in the Oxford English Dictionary which do not use any letters more than once, however, we will very gladly leave that challenge to the computer buffs.

Fill in the spaces to find the words. All letters are in the correct order and the overlapping letter appears twice.

**(a) 16-letter word.

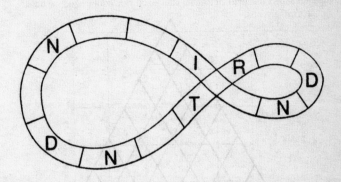

**(b) 13-letter word.

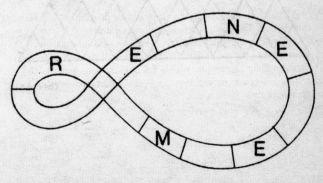

(See A94)

Using the following letters only, fill in the pyramid so that each horizontal line forms a word. Use each letter as many times as necessary. Each word formed must consist of same letters as word above it, in any order, plus one additional letter. (9-letter base.)

C, E, I, N, O, P, R, T

(See A31)

Place each of the 26 letters of the alphabet into the grid once only to form a crossword.

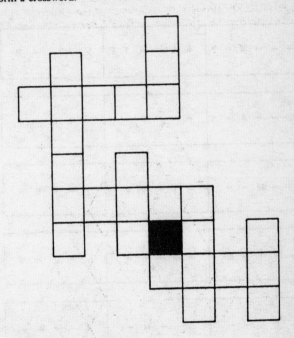

CLUES (in no particular order)

Animal
Fluent
Hit high
Nervous
Immoral practice
Stone of pure crystalline silica
Strap
Beaded moisture

(See A89)

Fill in the spaces to find the missing words. There is only one correct answer.

– – – E –	– L – – T	– A – – R
S – – A –	– – – P –	– L E – –
– – M – –	– I – R –	T – – E –
– – I – E	– M – – –	– – L – S
– I L – –	S – – N –	– – – K –
– E S – –	– T – E –	– R – – –

(See A93)

Using the following letters only, fill in the pyramid so each horizontal line forms a word. Use each letter as many times as necessary. Each word formed must consist of same letters as word above it, in any order, plus one additional letter. (10-letter base.)

A, B, D, E, I, L, R, T

(See A75)

Fill in the missing letters and find the nine-letter words.

(a)

A	T	
T	E	A
I		L

(b)

N	A	
	R	E
I	P	

(c)

	L	O
S	E	
I		K

(d)

M		O
E		R
	R	A

(e)

E		C
	N	U
I	S	

(See A5)

Place each of the 26 letters of the alphabet into the grid once only to form a crossword.

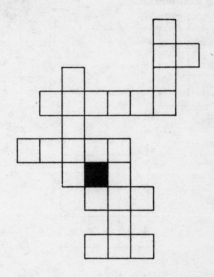

CLUES (in no particular order)

Across

Liquid measurement
Distress
Denoting ownership
Legendary maidens
Child

Down

Numerical indication
'H'-shaped
Pieces of work

(See A76)

CODES

Codes aren't everyone's cup of tea but they can be interesting in moderation. There is a fun code to start with and then they become progressively more difficult.

Ale Inn Cann's Code

A famous American, during the Civil War, used his own very special code when sending messages. He used the signature "ALE INN CANN" instead of his usual signature which was, of course, A. Lincoln. The sound was exactly the same but the words were different. If that's clear then try decoding the following cryptograms based on the same code which could have been sent by certain famous historical characters.

**(a) K. wee Nell is a bath spa knees are madder deaf it head barque Sue Noon wit trees or France est Dr. Ache.

**(b) Mr K. Ant any mill K. Mandy live red plea said rope bite on hight hand screw rub M. high B. hack K. Lee hope hat, Hoorah!

(See A83)

(a) $C_{18}V_2C_{99}$ $C_3V_4C_{11}V_2$!

$C_{10}V_2C_{15}15V_1C_5V_2$

$C_{15}V_5C_{22}V_2C_{15}154V_5C_{99}20$

$C_3V_2C_2V_4C_3V_2C_3$

***(b)** 72   11212   785   381313125   62129556   1082
8195   3556595554   31795171212 (?),   72
453245   7896   13566175,   3217517812179216!

(See A18)

XCNAWQ XU AHIWXAON HUJKGI GIXXIC EUCHL
MWH ZUYYUW IWHAWQL LJZR ML 'IC' MWH 'AWQ'
ZMW KI UO ZUWLAHICMKGI MLLALXMWZI ERIW
MXXIYFXAWQ XU HIZUHI YILLMQIL UO XRAL XNFI.
MHHAXAUWMG AWOUCYMXAUW, OUC ISMYFGI,
TWUEAWQ XRMX XRI GIXXIC 'I' AL XRI YULX
ZUYYUW GIXXIC AW XRI IWQGALR GMWQJMQI MWH
XRMX 'AWQ' AL XRI YULX ZUYYUW XRCII GIXXIC
EUCH IWHAWQ AL MGLU EUCXR TWUEAWQ.

(See A79)

BEYOND YOUR KEN?

Ken Russell, the Puzzle Editor of *Mensa*, the journal of British Mensa, always includes a 'Kickself' puzzle in his monthly column. Several of the puzzles included in this chapter are in the same spirit and if you don't solve them you may wish to kick yourself once you know the answer.

Missing Squares

Find the missing squares.

**(a)

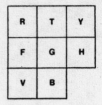 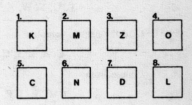

*(b)

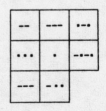 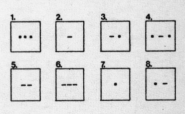

(See A74)

*(a) The following car licence plate is incomplete:

ROY   GB   I

To complete the plate choose one of the following:

T, U, V, W, X, Y, Z

**(b) Find the next to complete the sequence.

C, A, J, A, C, ?

Choose from:

A, C, L, J, P, V.

(See A63)

***(a) Without using either multiplication or division find out *quickly* which of the following numbers can be divided exactly by eleven:

(1) 504856

(2) 358938

(3) 8679

(4) 920986

(5) 3105

*(b) Find two 15-letter words which apart from the initial letter are spelt exactly the same.

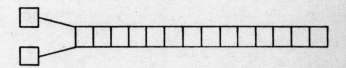

*(c) Show how $14^2 - 3^2 = 187$, without actually squaring either the 14 or the 3.

(See A35)

Remember Phil and Ken? They are now fitting a door to house number 73413. Ken threw out the challenge this time and asked Phil if he could screw all the digits to the door to display a number which could not be divided by 3. Could it be done?

(See A4)

Find the missing square.

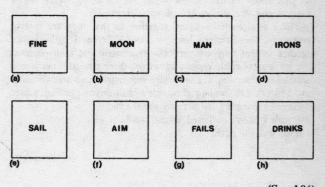

Choose from:

FINE (a)	**MOON** (b)
MAN (c)	**IRONS** (d)
SAIL (e)	**AIM** (f)
FAILS (g)	**DRINKS** (h)

(See A86)

There's no doubt it sure is a zzz,
Hit it now or give it a pass,
    Soon xxxxx to its charms,
    Never tire pulling arms,
Dare you give it a spin; xzzxxzxx?

(See A92)

***100
The Birthday Present

My wife asked me what I was buying her for her birthday. Never liking to give straightforward answers I replied:

   'Three straight lines joined together so that they are rotated symmetric, four straight lines of three different lengths joined together so that they are vertically symmetric and then repeated later on, a semi-circle repeated later on, three straight lines joined together so that they are vertically symmetric, two straight lines joined together to form a right-angle and three straight lines joined together so that they are laterally symmetric.'

   'I wish I hadn't bothered asking,' said my wife.

   What was the gift?

(See A30)

MENTAL EXERCISES

Variety is the spice of life and our aim in putting together this compilation has been to include as wide a selection of different types of puzzles and of as varying degrees of difficulty, as possible. This section is designed to exercise your mind and, maybe, to give you some inkling of how our own devious minds work.

(a) What letters complete these sequences?   (See A209)

    * (i)   M, V, E, M, J, S, U, N, ?

    * (ii) C, D, I, L, M, V, ?

  ** (iii) P, W, E, L, G, A, ?

(b) What is the next letter in this sequence?   (See A167)

    * O, T, F, S, N, E, T, F, S, N, T, T, ?

(c) What vowels complete these sequences?   (See A118)

  *** (i) E, OAE, EO, EE, UE, IIO, ?

   ** (ii) UA, OA, UEA, EEA, UA, IA, ?

(d) Should the letter K go above or below the line?   (See A131)

    ☆ A   E F   H I
           B C D   G   J

(e) Fill in the missing letters.   (See A143)

(a) Work out the missing numbers.   (See A145)

   * (i)   4, 9, 25, 49, 121, 169, 289, 361,
            ?, ?, 961

    * (ii) 97376, 7938, 1512, ?

    * (iii) 1, 4, 27, 256, ?

   ** (iv) 33278, 9436, 4278, 2996, ?

 *** (v) 22196, 4294, 988, ?

(b) Consider the number 7731.   (See A214)

Now continue the sequence –

 *** 153, 193, 197, 353, 413, 419, 793, 797, 813,
     819, ?, ?

(c) Find a reason for arranging these numbers into   (See A103)
groups of three.

 ** 127, 196, 361, 414, 428, 533, 565, 566, 693,
    761, 775, 961.

(d) Work out the missing number.   (See A227)

* **(a)** What do these words have in common? (See A162)

  STUDIO, CALMNESS, FIRST, INOPERATIVE, DEFEND.

* **(b)** *DESTRUCTION* IS TO *RUIN* AS *INSTRUCTOR* IS TO: (See A117)

  TEACHER, TUTOR, TRAINER, COACH, EDUCATOR.

*** **(c)** Consider the following list of words: (See A121)

  RACK, ON, GAIN, RAGE, ROW.

  Now choose one of the following words to add to the list:

  HEDGE, WOOD, STORM, TRACK, MAID, WATER, MILK.

** **(d)** Fill in the missing letters and read clockwise (See A220) to find the eight-letter words:

(i)   (ii)   (iii)

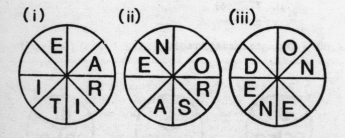

** (a) A wheel is spun containing 10 red and 10 (See A181)
yellow equal segments. Above the wheel is an
arrow. What are the chances that in any 10
consecutive spins the colour red will appear
against the arrow?

 * (b) Eight bingo balls numbered from 1 to 8 are (See A158)
placed into a bag then drawn out at random,
one by one, and the numbers written down to
form an eight-figure number. What are the
odds that the eight-figure number will divide
by 9 exactly?

 * (c) If the man who always transgressed against (See A212)
divine or moral law was named Dennis, the
girl who always felt unwell was named Delia,
and the lady who had a thing of value was
named Tessa, what was the name of the man
who carried a bag of letters?

 * (d) Jim, Alf and Sid each win on the horses for (See A194)
three days running. The following are the
nine amounts which the bookie paid out
(starting with the largest amount through to
the smallest amount).

£65 – £52 – £47 – £39 – £26 – £23 – £21 – £15
– £12.

Jim won twice as much as Sid but £20 less
than Alf. What was the total winning
amount for each man over the three days?

PUZZLES OF THE MIND

All the puzzles in this section consist entirely of diagrammatic representation. To solve them you have to apply your mind to each set of diagrams, comprehend the experience before you, and decide what logical patterns and/or sequences are occurring. The puzzles here are not ones of numeracy or literacy but are purely exercises of the mind, designed to test raw intelligence, free from the influence of prior knowledge.

We have shown several examples of the type of diagrammatic exercises used in intelligence tests – matrices, advanced matrices – conditions, but have devised all the exercises specially for this book, so that they are all original and not taken from actual intelligence tests.

Study the diagram and decide what logically should (See A132) be the missing section from the choices given.

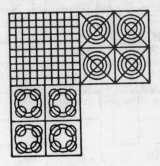

Choose from:

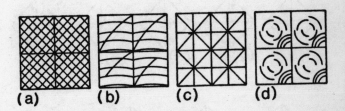

(a) (b) (c) (d)

Find the next figure: (See A215)

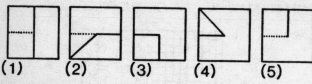

(1) (2) (3) (4) (5)

Choose from:

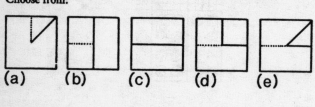

(a) (b) (c) (d) (e)

Find the next figure: (See A155)

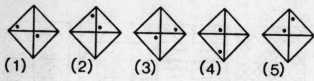

(1) (2) (3) (4) (5)

Choose from:

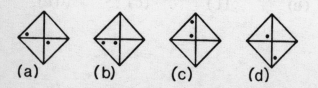

(a) (b) (c) (d)

Consider the three trominoes below: (See A189)

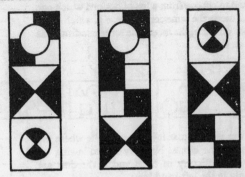

Now choose one of the following to accompany the above:

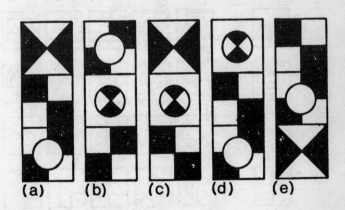

(a) **(b)** **(c)** **(d)** **(e)**

A condition is a test where you are shown one box and (See A201) then asked to choose from a list of options which one other box meets the same conditions, e.g. which of the five boxes on the right meets the same conditions as the box on the left.

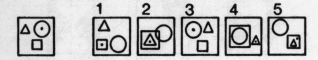

The answer is 3 because it is the only one where the dot is inside the circle. Now try the following (to increase the difficulty in A, B and E the dots are shown only in the left-hand box).

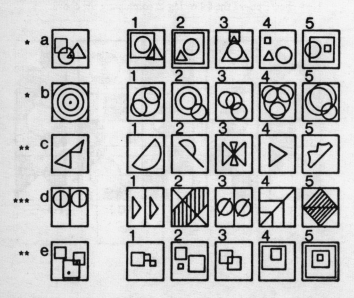

Look along each line horizontally, and then down (See A138) each line vertically to find what, logically, should be the missing square.

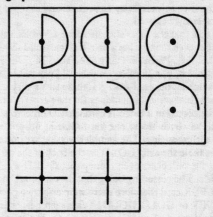

Choose from:

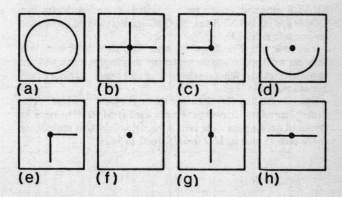

(a) (b) (c) (d)

(e) (f) (g) (h)

GAMBLING AND PROBABILITY

Man has always been a gambler. The urge to defeat the laws of probability is inherent in most people, although it was not until the 17th century, when Blaise Pascal, a French mathematician formulated the first rules relating to probability, that people were really aware that they existed.

It was in 1654 that the Chevalier de Méré asked Pascal why he lost when he bet even money that a pair of sixes would show once in 24 rolls of the dice. Pascal demonstrated that 24 rolls would be against the gambler, but 25 rolls could be slightly in his favour.

In America during the gold-rush era, there was a very ingenious gambling game that won a lot of money for the perpetrators. Three cards would be placed in a hat: one card GOLD on both sides, one card SILVER on both sides, one card GOLD on one side and SILVER on the other side. The gambler would take one card and place it on the table showing GOLD on the back of the card. Then he would bet the onlookers even money that GOLD would be on the reverse side. The reasoning being that the card could not be the SILVER/SILVER card therefore there were only two possibilities GOLD/SILVER or GOLD/GOLD. A fair even bet, or is it? The catch is that we are dealing in *sides* not cards. We start with six sides, three gold and three silver. We eliminate the SILVER/SILVER card and we can see one GOLD side. That leaves two GOLD and one SILVER unseen. Odds are therefore 2-1 on that the reverse side is GOLD.

The basic rule is really quite simple. Calculate the chances that an event will happen and then calculate the chances that it will not happen. Example: What are the odds against drawing a named card out of a pack of 52?

The probability of drawing the right card is 1/52. The probability of not drawing the right card is 51/52. The odds in favour of drawing the right card is the ratio of the first probability to the second, that is, 1/52 to 51/52, or 1 to 51.

(See A105)

A friend of yours is tossing a coin and you are betting him on the outcome. You bet on heads every time. Your unit stake is £1 per toss. You begin by betting £1 on the first toss. If you win, you again place £1 on the second toss but if you lose you double the stake to £2 then £4 and continue to double after every loss. After every win you revert to the £1 stake. After 100 tosses of the coin, heads has come down 59 times. How much profit are you making, assuming that the one-hundredth toss was heads?

*112

Typist

(See A202)

A typist types four envelopes and four letters. She places the letters in the envelopes at random. What are the chances that only three letters are in their correct envelopes?

(See A110)

A hand in bridge in which all 13 cards are a nine or below is called a Yarborough, after the second earl of Yarborough (d.1897), who is said to have bet 1000 to 1 against the dealing of such a hand. What, however, are the actual odds against such a hand? Was the noble lord onto a good thing?

**114
Probability Paradox

(See A164)

Four balls are placed in a hat. One is yellow, one is blue and the other two are red. The bag is shaken and someone draws two balls from the hat. He looks at the two balls and announces that one of them is red. What are the chances that the other ball he has drawn out is also red?

Lucky Card

(See A114)

In a competition each person receives a card with a number of rub-off pictures. One picture is marked loser, and only two pictures are identical. If the two pictures which are identical appear before the picture marked loser appears, then the competitor wins a prize.

There are 60 pictures on the card – what are the odds against winning?

Snooker

(See A144)

The game of snooker is played with 15 red balls, a black, a pink, a blue, a brown, a green, a yellow, and a white ball, which is the cue ball. Apart from the reds, which form a triangle at the top of the table, and the white, each of the remaining six coloured balls must be placed on its own spot on the table.

Two novices were setting up their first-ever game. They knew where to place the red balls and the cue (white) ball, but hadn't a clue which coloured ball went on which spot so decided to guess and spot the balls anywhere. How many possible different ways are there of spotting the six coloured balls?

CROSSWORDS

On Sunday 21 December 1913 the first crossword puzzle appeared in the *New York World*. It was devised by Liverpool-born Arthur Wynne, who called it a Word Cross Puzzle. That very first puzzle has since been reproduced exactly in several publications, but what we have done here is to create a completely new puzzle, using Arthur Wynne's original grid, but with an entirely different set of clues and answers. This tribute to Arthur Wynne is our first crossword puzzle in this set.

Based on first crossword by Arthur Wynne. (See A102)

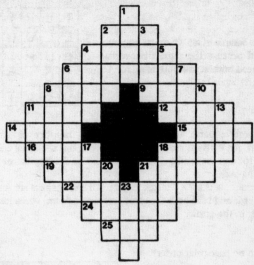

Across

2. Human Being (3)
4. Give Rise To (5)
6. Assembled (7)
8. Animal (4)
9. Vivacity (4)
11. Actor's Part (4)
12. Falsehoods (4)
14. Greek Letter (4)
15. Marsh Plant (4)
16. Adorn (4)
18. Adjacent (4)
19. Page (4)
21. Imitates (4)
22. Parts of Coat (7)
24. Parts of Body (5)
25. Not High (3)

Down

1. Story (4)
2. Only (4)
3. Knob (4)
4. Expose (4)
5. Explain (4)
6. Spacious Buildings (7)
7. Milk Suppliers (7)
8. Inn (5)
10. Requires (5)
11. Colour (3)
13. Look with Eyes (3)
17. Vegetable (4)
18. Spill Out (4)
20. Tumbled (4)
21. Profess (4)
23. Made of Ebony (4)

(See A182)

T	E	P	I	D
E	L	U	D	E
P	U	P	I	L
I	D	I	O	T
D	E	L	T	A

This is a sample of a 5×5 magic square, so called because the same five words can be read both across and down.

Magic-word squares become rarer as the number of letters increases. An 8×8 square has been compiled, but so far not a 9×9 or 10×10, and we doubt if one is possible in the English or any other language.

This example is a 7×7 magic square. All the answers are seven-letter words and read both the same across and down, when placed correctly in the grid.

Clues (In no particular order)

Devour Greedily

False to his Allegiance

Lamp

Settles

Stricter

One who enters Profession

Eccentric

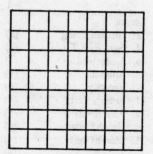

Answers run in the direction of compass points.   (See A238)

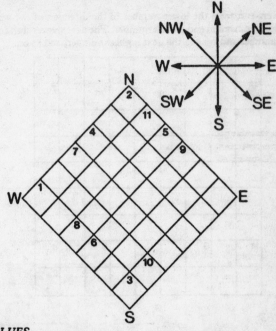

CLUES

1.E.	Palatable Liquids	5.W.	Exist
1.S.E.	Musical Piece	5.S.	Pain
1.N.E.	Harsh	6.N.	Before
2.S.	Errors	6.E.	Consumed
2.S.E.	Rubs Out	7.E.	Animal Doctors
3.N.E.	Spies	7.S.	Vehicle
4.E.	Age	8.E.	Midday
4.S.	Volcano	9.S.	Money
4.S.W.	Evenings	10.N.E.	Males
4.N.E.	Sooner Than	11.S.E.	Burns to the Ground

Criss-Cross

(See A141)

Answers run from the lower number in the direction of the next highest number and end on that number. The next answer starts on that number and runs to the next highest number, and so on.

CLUES

1. Expressed in Pictures (9)
2. Pair of Eye Glasses (9)
3. Tending to Expand (9)
4. Bring About (8)
5. Kidney Shaped (8)
6. Small Quantity (7)
7. Covered (7)
8. Slobber (5)

9. Lazily Reclining (7)
10. Hot Springs (7)
11. Exchanging for Money (7)
12. Pleased (4)
13. Given Medicine (5)
14. Beaded Moisture (3)
15. Used to be (4)
16. Dash (4)
17. Incline Head (3)

(See A126)

Complete the crossword, using the eight clues contained in the narrative below. Having solved the clues, place the answers in the correct position in the grid.

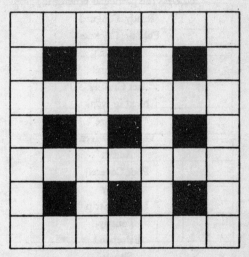

Doctor Foster who was a person skilled at operating, and of great standing posture, went to Gloucester by devious and roundabout ways, in a violent storm which had a rotary motion, on a dark overcast day. Whilst studying some aimless scrawls he stepped in a no longer used quarry right up to his middle and was not up to the occasion.

Insert the 26 letters of the alphabet into each grid once (See A204) only. Only one word is common to both grids.

CLUES (no particular order/grid)
Ready Tongued
Fold or Thickness
Approach
A Mineral
Act Craftily
Next in Rank
Moisture
Vault of Heaven
Addict
Foot Covered
Annoy
Leather Strip
Touchy
Falsehood
Shoots

Grid One   *Grid Two*

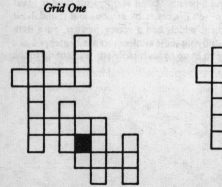
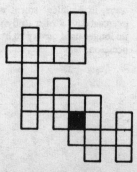

Here are five connected 5×5 magic squares. Answers (See A160) are all five-letter words and in each of the five grids read the same both across and down.

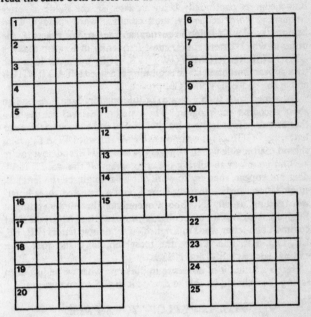

CLUES

1. Faded
2. Sky Blue
3. Money
4. Made Mistakes
5. Actions
6. Swap
7. Made Angry
8. Excuse
9. Sum Owed
10. Shortens
11. Express
12. Teacher
13. Make Amends
14. Medicine
15. Set Upright
16. Shot at Billiards
17. Pains
18. Makes Purchases
19. Colour
20. Composition
21. Vagabond
22. Runner
23. Sharp
24. Gives Out
25. Force

CRYPTOGRAMS

Cryptographers have at their disposal so much information on things like letter and word frequency that they will find the task of decoding the messages in this section extremely simple. Knowledge is continually being updated in the fields of letter frequency, word frequency, most common word endings, word beginnings, double-letter frequency, and so on. For example, the order in which letters appear most frequently in English today is ETAOINSRHLDCUMFPGWYBVKXJQZ; the order in which they appear most often at the beginning of a word is TAOSIWHCB and at the end ESDTNRYO.

So, armed with such a wealth of information, how does one go about decoding a cryptogram? The easiest to deal with are the ones that contain a four-letter word that begins and ends with the same letter, eg. FGHF. This is almost certainly the word THAT, which should then enable you to discover the word THE, and now you're well on your way to solving the cryptogram. If the word THAT does not appear, then try to work out what might be the letter E, single-letter words – usually A or I, and a repeated three-letter-word ending, usually ING (the most common three-letter ending in English). Also look for other obvious words such as AND; the most common two-letter word in English – OF, double letters (EE, FF, LL, OO, RR, and SS are the most common); and four-letter endings such as LESS and NESS.

Here's a little bit of nonsense to illustrate what we've just been saying. You should be able to decode it in about two minutes:

> 'FLOP LOPY PLOP?' YOWS TWEE.
> 'PLU KEOP LOP', YOWS TUG.
> 'IL PLOP LOP,' YOWS TWEE.
> 'PLOPY PLOP PLUG'.   (See A104)

The majority of cryptograms are straightforward simple types, where each letter of the alphabet is substituted for another, and there is only one message to be decoded. But what if the sender of the message wishes to convey a further message within the same cryptogram? This is done by the addition of keywords, which may be hidden in either the plain or the keyed text. As all the cryptograms which appear in this section have keywords or keyed phrases, we can show how these are uncovered by means of the following comment from Oliver Hardy, which he made to explain why he thought people found the L & H partnership so funny. (There is a further quotation keyed 5-2-4-8 by Henry Ward Beecher.)

G I.ZOKK GI BRK SOPRZKO BO BOHO KM PMFXWOIOWD ZQWGVO GQ OAOHD BRD. SZI WGVO SRPMQ RQN OLLK BO KOOFON IM SO RSMZI XOHTOPI IMLOIJOH — SZI QMI KM LMMN RXRHI.

This is simple substitution cryptogram, where one letter of the alphabet has been substituted for another, and is therefore deciphered in the usual way to arrive at the answer.

I GUESS IT WAS BECAUSE WE WERE SO COMPLETELY UNLIKE IN EVERY WAY. BUT, LIKE BACON AND EGGS, WE SEEMED TO BE ABOUT PERFECT TOGETHER — BUT NOT SO GOOD APART.

To find the keyed quotation place the code text in juxtaposition to the plain text, thus:

(PLAIN TEXT) A B C D E F G H I J K L M N O P Q R
(CODE TEXT)   R S P N O T L J G V W F Q M X H
(PLAIN TEXT) S T U V W X Y Z
(CODE TEXT)   K I Z A B D

As nothing appears yet which might look like a message, arrange the code text alphabetically in juxtaposition to the plain text:

(CODE TEXT)   A B C D E F G H I J K L M N O P Q R
(PLAIN TEXT) V W Y M I R T H S G O D E C N A
(CODE TEXT)   S T U V W X Y Z
(PLAIN TEXT) B F K L P U

Usually the keyword or, in this case, the keyed quotation, contains the only letters which do not appear in alphabetical order. By inspecting the plain text you may usually easily pick out where the alphabet appears in orderly succession and thus isolate the keyword letters. Above we see A to Y in order, thus suggesting the keyed quotation is contained in the letters MIRTHSGODECN. Because letters cannot be repeated in simple cryptograms the fun now begins if the keyed quotation repeats letters. It is therefore necessary to use your imagination to make sense of the message. In this case the answer is MIRTH IS GOD'S MEDICINE.

The addition of keywords has several purposes in addition to the practical one of sending an additional message which may escape the attention of an interceptor. It gives the compiler an opportunity to comment on the coded material, which is usually a quotation, and possibly display his own wit, or lack of it, and it adds an extra dimension to the puzzle.

Now try to decode the following cryptograms. Each letter of the alphabet is substituted by another, each cryptogram is in a different code, and each contains a keyword or phrase.

*124

Cryptogram (i)

Message keyed, 10-2-4-6   (See A135)

SNL NQGCF SHZC T MHTK GN JNY GSHG LSCF JNY SHZC

CDTETFHGCK GSC TEWNMMTODC, LSHGCZCI ICEHTFM,

SNLCZCI TEWINOHODC, EYMG OC GSC GIYGS?

                                    KNJDC

*125

Cryptogram (ii)

Message keyed, 4-3-4   (See A195)

ME MR SQAHQ EA ZPQJ ELPE HO QOON RAYMEFNO EA VMQN

AFDROYGOR. BODLPBR ME MR QAE RA HOYY SQAHQ ELPE

HO QOON RAYMEFNO EA VMQN AFD VOYYAHR OGOQ ELO

RPGMAFD MR NORUDMTON PR DOPULMQW ZPQSMQN

ELDAFWL ELO HMYNODQORR.

                              LPGOYAUS OYYMR

One word keyed, 12   (See A193)

HDHJKJOT KUL ALOAHKJNO NS H AUNMK AUHMY AUNQ.W,

SMNX H QULHY HOR QUJYYF QUNYYLM NO H PJT PIHQW

PINQW.

D. A. TJIPLMK

(KUL XJWHRN)

Message keyed, 5-2-10   (See A187)

JIXRSJK SH LH GLHC LH SX NIIUH. GZGFCXRSJK XLUGH

NIJKGF XRLJ CIY GBEGPX. SQ LJCXRSJK PLJ KI AFIJK,

SX ASNN MI HI; LJM LNALCH LX XRG AIFHX EIHHSONG

VIVGJX.

VYFERC'H NLA

'Listen, I don't mind you presenting taxing problems, BUT, do they have to be such frustratingly simple solutions? For the record, I hold you personally responsible for the bruises I inflicted on myself after seeing the solution to those groups of numbers each totalling 1000. Do you realise that all the raw unharnessed brainpower failing on that one could possibly run a nuclear reactor for a year at least?

'P.S. Please send me a photograph of yourself superimposed on a dartboard.'

So wrote one Mensa member recently after failing to solve one particular Kickself puzzle.

Each month a Kickself puzzle appears in *Mensa*, the Journal of British Mensa with a small prize for the first correct entry drawn out. You will be amazed at the trouble some members will take to submit solutions. We have had instances of solutions posted by special delivery at a cost exceeding the prize on offer, but the classic story is of the member who, armed with what he thought was the correct solution, cycled to the puzzle editor's home in Kent and arrived in the early hours of the morning. He had pedalled furiously all the way from the Isle of Dogs in Essex, a journey of some three hours, but was told, on arrival, that the answer he was proudly clutching was, in fact, the wrong solution!

This was my old telephone number.   (See A111)
What does it remind you of?

(314) 159 – 2654

Base to explorer at the South Pole: (See A184)

'What's the temperature?'
'Minus 40°' said the explorer.
'Is that Centigrade or Fahrenheit?' asked base.
'Put down Fahrenheit,' said the explorer. 'I don't expect it will mattter.'

Why did he say that?

Where would you place 9 and 10 to keep the sequence   (See A192)
going?

$$\frac{1 \quad 2 \qquad\qquad 6}{\quad 3 \ 4 \ 5 \quad 7 \ 8}$$

What is the next logical number in this sequence?   (See A136)

$$3, \quad 7, \quad 10, \quad 11, \quad 12, \quad ?$$

*132
Product

Find the product of: (See A113)
$$(x-a) \ (x-b) \ (x-c) \ \ldots \ (x-z)$$

***133
Calculate It

Why does $(12570 + 0.75) \times 16 \div 333$ = An animal?   (See A218)

(See A115)

I floated a lump of metal in a plastic bowl in a bath of water. Then I took the lump of metal out and dropped it into the water. Did the water level rise, fall, or remain the same?

**135
The Barrel of Rum Puzzle

(See A237)

'This barrel of rum is more than half full,' said Charlie. 'No it's not,' said Harry. 'It's less than half full.'

Without any measuring implements how could they easily determine who was correct? There was no lid on the barrel and no rum was taken out.

(See A200)

Fill in the missing numbers:

4	7	8	3	8	5
6	5			7	4
8	1	8	6	2	
3	6	5	8	7	6
	7	2	6	3	7
8	4	7	4	7	5

***137
Palindrome

(See A154)

Change the position of *one* number only to make this a palindromic sequence:

1, 4, 2, 9, 6, 1, 5, 10, 4

(See A134)

This is a true incident. See if you can figure out what actually happened.

Our golf club car park slopes steeply from south to north and the cars park in a vee-shape facing north (down-hill), as shown in the diagram.

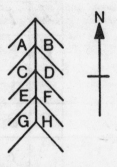

Recently two friends arrived for a four-ball and parked in spaces C and F. About two hours later, whilst they were halfway through their round, the club secretary went onto the course to tell them that the car in space F had just rolled forward into the one in space C.

Both cars were in perfect order, had no defects, and no one or nothing had pulled or pushed either car or had tampered with them in any way. What is the explanation?

(See A120)

Two strangers enter a pub. The publican asks them what they would like. First man says, 'I'll have a bottle of stout,' and puts 50p down on the counter. Publican: 'Guinness at 50p, or Jubilee at 45p?' First man: 'Jubilee'. Second man says, 'I'll have a bottle of stout,' and puts 50p on the counter. Without asking him the publican gives him Guinness. How did he know what he required?

(See A217)

Man calls to waiter in the restaurant, 'There's a fly in my tea'. 'I will bring you a fresh cup of tea,' says the waiter. After a few moments the man calls out, 'This is the same cup of tea!' How did he know?

(See A112)

Study the numbers in each horizontal line and then decide what, logically, should be the missing numbers.

| 3 3 1 | 2 3 1 1 | 1 2 1 3 2 1 |

| 2 3 3 | 1 2 2 3 | 1 1 2 2 1 3 |

| 1 2 1 | 1 1 1 2 1 1 | |

(See A205)

What letter completes this sequence?

AEEOEEIEUE?

Do you find solving anagrams as 'INCOMPREHENSIBLE' as solving a 'PROBLEM IN CHINESE'? Do you know a 'ONE WORD' anagram for 'NEW DOOR'? 'NOR DO WE'!

Anagrams were invented by the Greek poet Lycophon in AD 280. Originally an anagram was simply a word which when reversed formed another word. For example, ROOM/MOOR, or TIDE/EDIT. The word, 'anagram' is derived from Greek: 'ANA' means 'backwards' and 'GRAMMA' 'a letter'.

The best anagrams are those where the rearranged letters bear some relationship to the original word or name; for example, the letters of the word 'SOFTHEARTEDNESS' can be rearranged to form the phrase 'OFTEN SHEDS TEARS'.

For hundreds of years compilers have tried to find hidden meanings in rearranging the names of famous people. Some of our favourites are: 'I'LL MAKE A WISE PHRASE' (WILLIAM SHAKESPEARE), 'ON THEN, O SAILOR' (HORATIO NELSON), 'FLIT ON CHEERING ANGEL' (FLORENCE NIGHTINGALE) and 'OUR BEST NOVELS IN STORE' (ROBERT LOUIS STEVENSON). Politicians too inevitably find their names being rearranged into appropriate phrases. Depending on your point of view, 'MARGARET THATCHER' is either 'THAT GREAT CHARMER' or 'MEG THE ARCH TARTAR'; 'RONALD REAGAN' is 'LOAN ARRANGED'; and the former British prime minister 'WILLIAM EWART GLADSTONE' becomes 'WILD AGITATOR MEANS WELL'.

Before you tackle the host of anagrams that follow we will leave one particularly tricky little teaser with you. Rearrange the letters of the words 'ROAST MULES' to form a single 10-letter word. It is a common English word, with which everyone is familiar, but it is surprisingly very difficult to find (see A123).

All these are one-word anagrams: (See A161)

(a) EASTER EGG   (f) BORDELLO
(b) IS A CHARM   (g) ADMIRER
(c) REMOTE   (h) INTO MY ARM
(d) OPEN CLAIM   (i) THERE WE SAT
(e) HOTEL SUITE   (j) RESTFUL

***144
Swop Round

(See A233)

Change the numbers to letters to find three 9-letter words:

1 2 3 4 5 6 7 8 9

2 3 1 4 5 6 7 8 9

8 9 3 1 2 4 5 6 7

(See A109)

Each word or phrase in quotation marks is an anagram of another word. The solution bears some relationship to the original.

(a) 'UP CLOSE' 'TRIFLING'   (7/8)

ANSWER: '_____', '_____'

(b) 'EMIT GRUNT' through 'MOUTH CASE'   (9/9)

ANSWER: '_____' through '_____'

* (a) All American presidents: (See A190)
     (i)   OH! GOING? GREAT NEWS
     (ii)   RAM BALL ON CHAIN
     (iii) BOTH HERE ROVER
     (iv)   WIND OR OWLS WOO
     (v)   LODGE CIVIC LOAN
     (vi)   O DO REVERSE THE TOOL
     (vii) A FOOLER SENT LINK OVERLAND

** (b) All well-known writers: (See A179)
     (i)   KEN SCARES CHILD
     (ii)   REASON ANN IT'S HARD CHINS
     (iii) LOB NET OR CHATTER
     (iv)   NEW SMILE ESSENTIAL
     (v)   A BELL CHARMS
     (vi)   TO STEER NOON SILVER BUS
     (vii) SHAME MARE MUST GO

(See A137)

You must enter each room once only in a continuous route and spell out a 15-letter word. You may enter the corridor as many times as you wish.

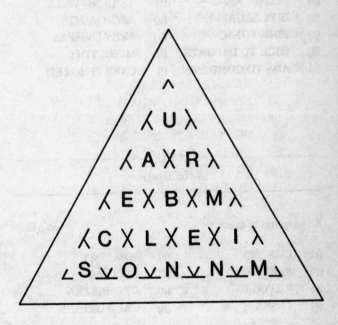

(See A186)

Antigrams are anagrams in which the letters of a word are reorganized to form a word or phrase meaning the opposite. Answers are one word.

(a) I LIMIT ARMS
(b) IS IT LEGAL? NO
(c) FINE TONIC
(d) NICE TO IMPORTS
(e) AIM TO CONDEMN
(f) TEAR NO VEILS
(g) ARCHSAINTS
(h) ARE ADVISERS
(i) MORE TINY
(j) CARE IS NOTED

*149
Animalgrams

All anagrams of animals.

(See A133)

(a) CORONA
(b) PAROLED
(c) RETIRER
(d) LESIONS
(e) SOMEDAY
(f) ALPINES
(g) ORCHESTRA
(h) CALIFORNIA†

†two words

In each of the following unscramble the letters to find a word. There are no two adjoining letters in the same shape.

* (a) 11-letter word. (See A106)

** (b) 12-letter word. (See A219)

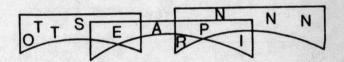

*** (c) 14-letter word. (See A163)

In each set below arrange the 14 words in pairs so that each pair is an anagram of another word or name. The seven words produced will have a linking theme. For example, if the words 'DIAL' and 'THAN' were in the list they could be paired to form an anagram of 'THAILAND' and the theme would be countries.

(a) AMPLE (See A157)
CAME
CARE
CENTRE
CHIN
COIN
CORD
CREASE
MORE
RAP
SHAKE
THE
TO
TRY

(b) FEED (See A140)
FRAIL
GAIN
GRIN
GRIP
HEAT
HERS
LAG
LAST
LOVE
PANS
TRADE
TRAMP
WAIT

It is interesting how some numbers have their own individual characteristics.

With some numbers it is possible to tell if they are a factor of a large number without having to do a division calculation. Examples of such numbers are 3, 9 and 11. With 3 and 9 all that is necessary is to total up the digits. If their sum is divisible by 3 or 9 then the number itself is divisible by 3 or 9, e.g. the sum of the digits 3912 is 15, which divides by 3 exactly. Therefore, the number 3912 or any combination of these digits also divides exactly by 3. Similarly the digits 497286 total 36, which divides by 9, so the number 497286 or any combination of these digits also divides exactly by 9.

The test for 11, which is not so well known, is to see if the separate sums of alternate digits are equal, e.g. the number 746218 is divisible by 11 exactly, when read either forward or backward, because $7 + 6 + 1 = 4 + 2 + 8$.

There is also a way of finding out if a number is divisible by 7 or 13. The system is the same for both 7 and 13 and it is to split the number into groups of three starting from the end and insert alternating minus/plus signs. For example, $587932 \times 7 = 4115524$ and $4 - 115 + 524 = 413$; therefore, because 413 is divisible by 7, so is 4115524; similarly $896712 \times 13 = 11657256$, so $11 - 657 + 256 = -390$ and as 390 is divisible by 13, so is 11657256.

Another interesting number is 37, because when multiplied it very often produces a palindromic number or, if not palindromic, a number which will divide by 37 when read forward or backward. The reason for this is simply that it is a third of the number 111, and we have illustrated its palindromic qualities later.

Somehow all the numbers mentioned above – 7, 9, 11, 13, 3, 37, (111) – seem to come together in the magic six digits 142857. This is the number which fascinated Charles Lutwidge Dodgson (1832-98), who was a lecturer in mathematics at Oxford from 1855 until 1881, but is better known as Lewis Carroll.

By dividing 1 by 7 we get the cyclical number 0.142857142857 and by multiplying together $3 \times 9 \times 11 \times 13 \times 37$ we get the same recurring digits 142857. Taking the same six digits Carroll discovered some fascinating characteristics.

TABLE ONE

$$142857 \times 1 = 142857$$
$$142857 \times 2 = 285714$$
$$142857 \times 3 = 428571$$
$$142857 \times 4 = 571428$$
$$142857 \times 5 = 714285$$
$$142857 \times 6 = 857142$$

The six digits always stay in the same order but move round each time so that each digit occupies each of the six positions. When multiplied by 7 the result is a row of six nines. If you add the first and last three digits the result each time is 999.

It was almost certainly this number that inspired the Mad Hatter's Tea Party, which illustrates the idea of cyclic order:

'Let's all move one place on'.

Like ourselves Carroll loved tinkering with words and numbers and inventing and solving puzzles. We don't know if he experimented further with his magic number, but we have done so, and by dividing each of the numbers in TABLE ONE by 3, 9, 11, 13, 37 and 111 in turn have arrived at the following results:

Table Two (÷3)	Table Three (÷9)	Table Four (÷11)
47619	15873	12987
95238	31746	25974
142857	47619	38961
190476	63492	51948
238095	79365	64935
285714	95283	77922

Table Five (÷13)	Table Six (÷37)	Table Seven (÷111)
10989	3861	1287
21978	7722	2574
32967	11583	3861
43956	15444	5148
54945	19305	6435
65934	23166	7722

Except for TABLE THREE, it can be seen that all the numbers in the other tables are linked in some characteristic way.

In TABLES ONE, TWO, FOUR and FIVE the sum of the digits of each number is 27. In TABLES SIX and SEVEN the sum of the digits of each number is 18. In TABLES FOUR and FIVE the middle digit of each number is 9. In TABLE FOUR the sum of the vertical second and fifth row of figures is 27. In fact, these vertical rows contain the magic digits 124578 but not in their cyclic order. IN TABLE SEVEN the numbers are the same as TABLE FOUR without the centre digit 9.

All this would have surely interested Carroll considerably, and no doubt he would have approved of the following curious little puzzle which we have devised to illustrate the palindromic qualities of the number 37.

**152
The Magic '37'

(See A191)

If the digits 1 – 9 are placed in the grid as follows:

4	6	2
7	1	9
8	5	3

a total of 16 different numbers will be formed if each horizontal, vertical and corner-to-corner line is read both forward and backward.

Rearrange the digits 1 – 9 in the grid in such a way that if each of the 16 three-figure numbers are extended to form a palindromic six-figure number (e.g. 462264 or 264462) then each of those 16 six-figure numbers will divide exactly by 37.

(See A107)

Place the digits into the grid in such a way that every horizontal and vertical line when read both forwards and backwards, and also the sum of the digits of every horizontal and vertical line, can be divided by nine exactly.

1, 1, 1, 2, 2, 2, 2,

3, 3, 4, 4, 5, 5, 6,

7, 7, 7, 7, 7, 7,

8, 8, 9, 9, 9.

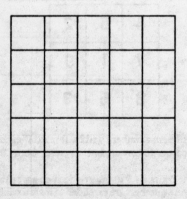

Place the digits into the grids so that each horizontal and vertical line is divisible by 11 exactly, when read either forwards or backwards. Remember, no multiplication or division is necessary. All you need to do is ensure that the alternate digits in each horizontal and vertical line when added together equal the same; for example, 5148, i.e. 5+4 = 1+8.

(a)   (See A213)

1, 1,

3, 3, 3, 3, 3,

4, 4, 5, 5,

6, 6, 8, 8, 9.

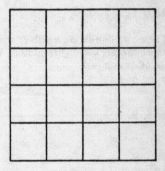

(b)   (See A203)

1, 1, 1,

2,

3, 3, 3, 3, 3,

4, 5, 5, 6, 7, 8, 9.

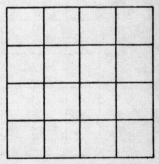

(a)   (See A139)

These two four-figure numbers share a feature in common
with only one other four-figure number. What is the feature
and what is the other number?

3600,   5776

(b)   (See A168)

These two four-figure numbers share a feature in common with
only one other four-figure number. What is the feature and what is
the other number?

2025,   9801

ODD ONE OUT (ii)

One of our very good friends in Enigmasig, Cynan Rees, once sent us an odd-one-out puzzle with a difference. He gave us a list of six words and asked us to make out a case for each of the words being the odd one out for a different reason. The words he presented us with were:

ABORT
ACT
AGT
ALP
OPT
APT

Can you find a reason for each of the words being the odd one out? (For answer see A146.) This puzzle is a fine example of the pitfalls which compilers must try to avoid. Hopefully all the puzzles which follow in this section will have just one clear reason why one only of the options given is the odd one out.

Sentences

(See A119)

Which one of these sentences is the odd one out?

(1) FRIENDSHIP LINGERS UNTIL THE END.

(2) LOVERS STROLL UNDER THE STARS.

(3) HEAVEN ALWAYS REPAYS PERFECTION.

(4) THE UPROAR BEGINS AGAIN.

**157
Words

In each of the following which is the odd one out?

(a)   (See A216)   (b)   (See A223)

DEBT	SING
AIM	RECORD
KNOW	TEAR
TWO	REBEL
SCENE	WIND
AEON	

(See A142)

Which of these figures is the odd one out?

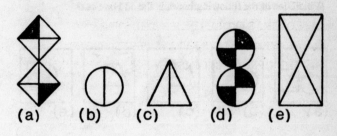

(a)   (b)   (c)   (d)   (e)

***159
Spot The Dot

(See A239)

One of the dots in this circle is an intruder. Which one?

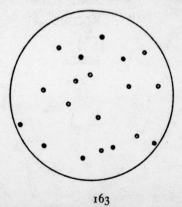

(See A156)

An intelligence test where you are shown a number of boxes and asked to choose the one which is different is called 'Classification'. Which one of the following boxes is the odd one out?

(a)　　　(b)　　　(c.)　　　(d)　　　(e)

(See A176)

Which of these four crosses is the odd one out?

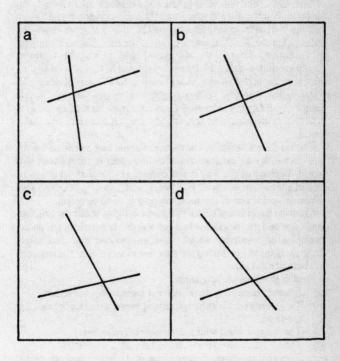

The English language, the most commonly spoken language in the world, has evolved from an awkward native dialect, the tongues of various invaders and the importation of other foreign words after the expansion of the British Empire.

The basic element of the English language is Teutonic, or German, and the dialects spoken by the various English and Saxon tribes which overran England during the fifth to seventh centuries belonged to the West Germanic group of the Indo-Germanic family of languages. To a basis of Anglo-Saxon words the Norman Conquest added many Norman-French words of Latin origin to which were added many more words from Latin during the Renaissance. Finally, with the great expansion of the British Empire, words were imported from countries such as India, and other terms introduced by sailors and travellers from all parts of the world.

The result is a language consisting of some half a million words and spoken by an estimated 400 million people throughout the world. Because of the way it has evolved the English language is rich in alternative words such as 'work' and 'labour', 'friendly' and 'amiable' and is one of the most expressive of all tongues.

Mensans never tire of discovering new delights about the English language and its treasure chest of words, and below are some examples of wordplay which have entertained and fascinated Enigmasig members during the past few months. (For the answers to these see A116.)

Find in the English language:

(a) A word containing three adjacent pairs of double letters.

(b) Two words which although antonyms are pronounced exactly the same.

(c) The longest word which does not repeat letters.

(d) Two 8-letter words which contain all 5 vowels.

(e) Two commonly used words, one of 11 letters and one of 13 letters, which start and finish with the same three letters in the same order.

(f) A 12-letter word having a 2:1 vowel to consonant ratio.

(g) The only word which has the letters 'GNT' in succession.

(h) An 8-letter word which forms another word when reversed.

(i) Four words containing all five vowels in the correct forward or reverse order.

Square Words

Spiral clockwise round the perimeter and finish at the centre square to spell out the nine-letter words. Each word commences at one of the four corner squares.

* (a) (See A211)

P	O	
E	E	
	E	T

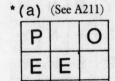

* (a) (See A211)

P		O
E	E	
	E	T

** (b) (See A180)

A		E
R	E	N
	M	

* (c) (See A128)

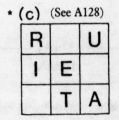

R		U
	I	E
	T	A

*** (d) (See A152)

	E	R
E	R	
R		O

** (e) (See A199)

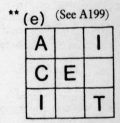

A		I
C	E	
I		T

(See A122)

Work from the top left-hand square to the bottom right, moving from square to square horizontally, vertically or diagonally to find five words. Every letter in the grid must be used once only.

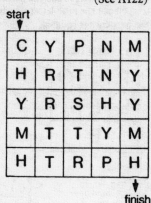

start

C	Y	P	N	M
H	R	T	N	Y
Y	R	S	H	Y
M	T	T	Y	M
H	T	R	P	H

finish

**164
Alphabet

Use the 26 letters of the alphabet once each to complete these words.

ABCDEFGHIJKLM
NOPQRSTUVWXYZ

(See A174)

1. — A - E
2. L - - - R I - -
3. Z - - E
4. - O U - -
5. - O Y
6. - Y - E
7. - E - R -
8. - - A - I - -
9. E - I - -

(See A169)

Here are two lists of words.

Each word in List A has two possible pair words in List B.
Each word in List B has two possible pair words in List A.

There are two possible solutions.
Pair a word from each list until you have 10 pairs.

List A	*List B*
SEVERN	TRACTOR
ARROW	RIVER
TURRET	BULL'S-EYE
FARM	BOW
YARBOROUGH	TANK
SAND	CARDS
YEW	CASTLE
VEHICLE	BANK
RIPARIAN	WOOD
JACK	BRIDGE

(See A224)

What have all the answers to the following clues in common?

1. DOCTRINE
2. FEELER
3. HOLDING FAST
4. FISH
5. OFFER
6. GAME
7. FRAME
8. THIN
9. MEANING
10. FIT FOR HABITATION

**167
Follow That

(See A178)

The following words are a logical progression:

THAT
DOCUMENTATION
MEANDER
GRAVY
EMBANKMENT
JUBILEE

Which is next – EXTERMINATION, OCCUPATION, GRAMMAR, or ZOO?

(See A171)

Each horizontal and vertical line includes the consonants of a word which can be completed by adding a number of 'U' vowels. The two-figure number at the end of each line indicates the number of consonants and 'U' vowels, e.g. 2-1 indicates two consonants and one 'U' vowel.

	1	2	3	4	5	6	7	
1	R	S	J	T	G	R	K	2·1
2	S	S	C	F	S	C	C	4·2
3	C	C	P	M	P	B	S	5·2
4	S	G	S	L	P	F	Z	2·2
5	C	R	B	S	M	S	C	5·3
6	M	C	C	F	L	S	C	4·3
7	T	T	P	S	T	F	H	3·1

4·1   3·2   3·1   4·1   3·1   3·1   4·1

Each letter in the grid is used once only and all letters must be used. (The consonants to be used in each line are not necessarily in the correct order or adjacent.)

CLUES

Across
1. CONTAINER
2. NORTH AFRICAN DISH
3. BE OVERCOME
4. BANTU
5. FEMALE DEMON
6. CLOUD
7. STRIKE GOLF BALL

Down
1. ROOF SUPPORT
2. SPIRITUAL TEACHERS
3. HORN OF CRESCENT
4. MATERIAL
5. LIGHT SHOE
6. BIRD
7. PART OF LATHE

(See A221)

Each of the sentences below contains, in the correct order, the letters of a word that is opposite to the meaning of the sentence, e.g. *CLOSE TO BOILING* = COOL.

Find the words:

(a) A HAVEN OF LOVELINESS
(b) NOT FOR SOME TIME OR MAYBE NEVER
(c) FROZEN, NOT OFF THE SHELF
(d) A GREAT EFFORT AND STILL FRESH ENOUGH TO DO IT OVER AGAIN
(e) PUT YOUR EFFORT IN SHIFTING IT TOWARDS US
(f) SEW IT VERY TIGHTLY TOGETHER
(g) A LOT OF COMPANY FOR ME
(h) HATED OR REVILED
(i) READ IN COMPLETE SILENCE TO YOURSELF
(j) INDELICATE, UGLY AND UNCULTURED
(k) TRUSTY, EVER SINCERE AND HONEST
(l) NEW AND INEXPERIENCED MEMBER OF OUR BODY AND PROFESSION
(m) RUN ALONG SPEEDILY IN THE RACE
(n) NOW STALE AND VERY WORN

(See A173)

Answers are all six-letter words. Pair up two sets of three letters to form the answer.

CLUES
1. SEAMEN'S CHURCH
2. ANIMATING SPIRIT
3. ALLIGATOR
4. KEPT IN THIRD PERSON'S CUSTODY
5. INSOLENT PRIDE
6. WATCH A GAME OF CARDS
7. FASHIONABLE
8. POROUS LAVA
9. FULL OF CHINKS
10. SMALL PERFUMED BAG
11. SWOLLEN
12. WHIMSICAL NOTION
13. SHELL MONEY
14. SLUGGISHNESS
15. GENTLE BREEZE
16. NECKLACE OF TWISTED METAL

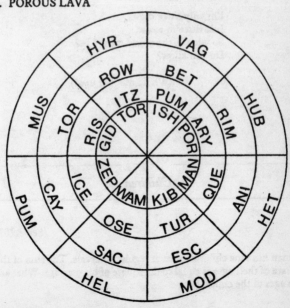

THE WORLD OF NUMBERS

Mathematics may be defined as the subject in which we never know what we are talking about, nor whether what we are saying is true.

Bertrand Russell

**171
Number Rhyme

(See A175)

If my three were a four,
And my one were a three,
What I am would be nine less
Than half what I'd be.

I'm only three digits,
Just three in a row,
So what in the world must I be?
Do you know?

(Whole number used)

***172
Children

(See A207)

A man has nine children born at regular intervals. The sum of the square of their ages is equal to the square of his own age. What are the ages of the children?

(See A124)

This field, 112 m × 75 m, can be split up into 13 square plots.
Fill in the dimensions.

All dimensions are in whole metres.

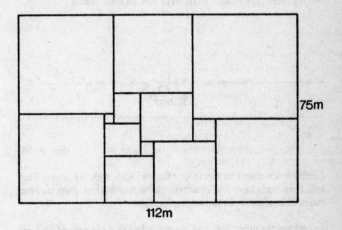

75m

112m

Not to scale

(See A172)

A sneak thief had been at work in the classroom. When the pupils returned from lunch 80 per cent had lost a pencil, 85 per cent had lost a pen, 74 per cent had lost a ruler and 68 per cent had lost a rubber.

What percentage at least must have lost all four items?

(See A188)

Coincidence seems to run in our family. Although my sisters Pam and Fran each have five children, twins and triplets, Pam had her twins first whereas Fran had triplets first.

I saw Pam the other day, and she remarked that the sum of the ages of her children was equal to the product of their ages. I pointed out that although interesting this was not unique, as Fran could say exactly the same about her children.

How old are my sisters' children?

**176
Fraction

(See A166)

Arrange the following digits, 1 – 2 – 3 – 4 – 5 – 6 – 7 – 8 - 9, to form a single fraction that equals one third.

**177
'100' Puzzle

(See A129)

Without changing the order of the digits form a calculation equal to 100. Only four plus and/or minus signs can be inserted between the digits.

$$9 \quad 8 \quad 7 \quad 6 \quad 5 \quad 4 \quad 3 \quad 2 \quad 1 \; = \; 100$$

*178
Zero

(See A210)

Without changing the order of the digits insert four plus signs, one division sign and three minus signs between them to make the calculation correct.

$$9 \quad 8 \quad 7 \quad 6 \quad 5 \quad 4 \quad 3 \quad 2 \quad 1 \; = \; 0$$

(See A150)

When the Roman army needed to punish a large number of men, every tenth soldier was executed – hence the word 'decimate'.

You are one of a band of 1,000 mutinous pirates, captured and tied to numbered posts arranged in a circle.

The first is to be executed, then each alternate pirate, until one remains, who will go free.

Which number post would you choose?

****180**
Decimal Points

(See A127)

In this addition sum, only one decimal point is in its correct position. Alter four of the decimal points to make the sum correct.

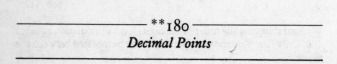

$$
\begin{array}{r}
36.7 \\
1874.5 \\
109.6 \\
14.8 \\
\hline
383.11
\end{array}
$$

Fifty-seven matchsticks are laid out to form the sum below, which is obviously incorrect.

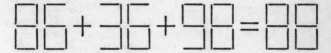

But by removing *two* matchsticks it is possible to make the sum correct:

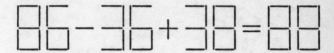

** (a) Now the same sum is again laid out, but this time remove *eight* matchsticks to make the sum correct. (Do not disturb the matchsticks already laid out, apart from the eight to be removed.)

(See A231)

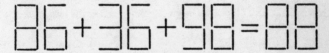

* (b) Now an incomplete sum. This time *add 18* matchsticks to make the sum correct. (Do not disturb the matchsticks already laid out.) This one is a kick-self.

(See A153)

Among the 10 quotations in this section we have selected three by William Shakespeare, including the first one, an acrostic.

Acrostic

(See A222)

Solve the clues, place each letter in its appropriate position in the grid, and a Shakespeare quotation will appear.

	1	2	3	4	5	6	7	8	9	10	11	12	13	14	15	16	17	18	19	20	21
A																					
B																					
C																					
D																					
E																					
F																					

Clue		
LING	(7)	2F 8B 2C 1E 12C 3F 18D
AVAILS ONESELF OF	(4)	13F 5F 12A 14E
REMAINS	(7)	15D 15B 10F 7B 19F 17F 7A
HAUGHTY	(6)	15C 21E 7E 15A 10B 13E
AMOUNTING TO	(10)	17B 16F 2B 14F 7D 4F 20E 14B 5B 5A
MUSCLE CRAMP	(7)	14C 7C 12E 10E 13B 9D 18F
SEEKS JUSTICE FROM	(4)	19D 17D 6F 17A
ENTRANCE.	(9)	20B 3C 16E 9A 11D 6A 16D 7F 6E
A CARDINAL NUMBER	(4)	3C 1B 12B 19C
GREAT HAPPINESS	(8)	1A 9C 17C 6B 1C 4B 3D 4E
BE OF VALUE	(5)	9E 8F 18E 1D 13A
FAINTS	(6)	19E 16A 2A 4D 2D 8A
LIFT UP	(7)	10D 6D 16C 18C 14D 11C 17E
FOAM	(5)	11A 3A 11B 1F 18B
DOES WRONG	(7)	12F 3B 20A 13C 20F 8D 20C
CUT WITH AXE	(3)	2E 9F 11E
OF THE THIGH	(7)	13D 3E 8C 19A 5C 19B 14A

In each of the following, two quotations are squashed together. All the letters are in the correct order. Find the two quotations. To assist, the authors' names follow the quotations but have been squashed together in the same way.

(See A130)

* (a) AALLLKLLENOARNWINLEDGGIESBIUSTBRUE
  TCREOMELMLBECRATNICOEN
  SPOCLRAATETOS

(See A177)

** (b) TOYOEUHARVETRWOEAISRSHEHARBUOTHMS
  IDANTESOFOFTORHEGIVQUEESDTIVIOINNE
  SPPOURGPEEON

In each of the following find the starting point, fill in the missing letters, and a quotation will appear. Then rearrange the missing letters to find the author/originator of the quotation.

*(a) Author (5 letters) (See A159)　　**(b) Author (6 letters)** (See A183)

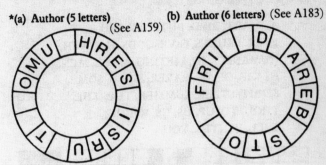

*(c) Originator (6,6) (See A165)

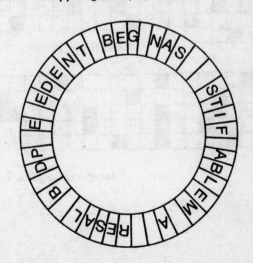

I'll Make a Wise Phrase

(See A125)

Place each word in the correct position in the correct grid and two Shakespeare quotations will appear.

A, A, ART, BIRD, BUT, DAY, DID,
EVER, FAULTS, GIVE, GODS, HAUNCH,
HUMANITY, IN, LIFTING, MAKE, MEN,
NEVER, OF, OF, RARER, SINGS, SOME,
SPIRIT, STEER, SUMMER, THE, THE,
THOU, TO, UP, US, US, WHICH,
WILL, WINTER, YOU.

King Henry IV, Part 2, IV. iv

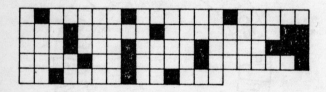

Antony and Cleopatra, V. i. 31

BRAINBENDERS FOR MENTALATHLETES

'It is quite a three-pipe problem.' – Sir Arthur Conan Doyle.

In this section we have chosen what we consider to be some of the more difficult problems, or, we should say, puzzles, in the book. Some time ago in *Mensa* (the magazine of British Mensa), Dr Madsen Pirie defined the difference between puzzles and problems. A puzzle, he said, is set by another person, and it has one solution, or more, which is already known by that person. It is a puzzle to ask 'Which three-digit number has the most factors?' (see A197) or 'What is the lowest number (apart from 0 and 1) that is a square number, a cube number, and a number to the 4th power, 5th power and 6th power?' (See A108). A problem, on the other hand, arises in life. It is not set artificially and there is not an answer already known by someone else. There is no right answer; some solutions may be better than others.

While both puzzles and problems bring their rewards some may prefer one to the other. Certainly the successful solution of a problem achieves a worthwhile goal and perhaps the major benefit to be obtained from tackling puzzles is that they stretch and exercise the mind and enable you to tackle the real problems of life with renewed vigour and confidence.

***186
Categorize

(See A236)

Arrange the following into groups of three:

ARQUEBUS
ATOLL
BOARD
CANAL
DOOR
FIELD
FLINTLOCK
GUN
ISLET
KEY
NOTE
STONE

****187
Odd One Out

(See A170)

Which is the odd one out and why?

CHIS
DENC
FRAP
PERL
PORL
SPAD

(See A229)

A 2½in. square card is thrown at random onto a tiled floor. What are the odds against its falling not touching a line?

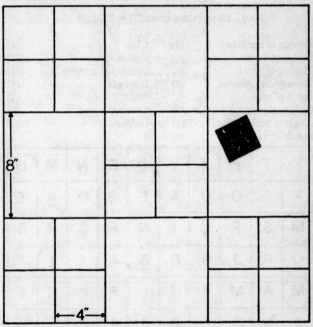

You should assume that the pattern repeats over a large area.

(See A232)

Answers will be found in letter order in the grid. Use every letter in the grid once each only:

(e.g.) Elastic-sided boots (7) = JEMIMAS

Disease of the skin	(5)	Clan	(4)
Dance of death	(7)	Cotton fabric	(9)
Mother-of-pearl	(5)	Student of archery	(11)
Rectangular column	(8)	Inert gas	(5)
Force of men	(5)	Veil	(7)
Chip basket	(6)	Lettered board	(5)
Angle of building	(5)	Colour	(5)
Shrub	(6)		

X	T	P	J	Y	O	S	N	M	O
X	A	O	U	A	E	E	O	A	E
M	S	P	C	I	N	P	C	P	S
O	R	J	H	P	S	A	I	I	T
M	A	M	B	U	L	E	A	N	E
Z	N	Q	L	A	S	A	A	R	H
E	U	I	K	U	A	N	E	S	S
L	O	I	P	T	E	P	L	V	E
L	I	U	T	I	T	E	V	E	E
A	R	T	A	E	N	E	E	S	N

How many triangles are there in each of the following figures? The number of triangles increases in each figure. The first figure is a warm-up.

*(a) (See A208) ***(b) (See A196)

***(c) (See A147) ***(d) (See A226)

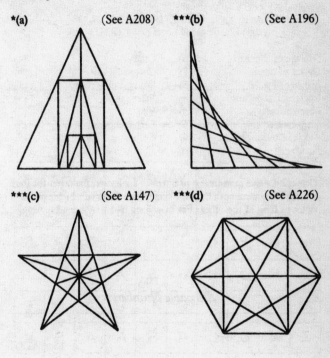

(See A198)

What is the next number in this sequence, and why?

1, 4, 7, 11, 15, 18, 21, 24, 27, ?

***192
Candles

(See A151)

One candle was guaranteed to burn for six hours, the other for four hours. They were both lit at the same time. After some time one was twice as long as the other. For how long had they been burning?

****193
Amicable Numbers

(See A235)

These are rare numbers. They are	?	?
pairs of numbers where the sum of	1184	1210
the factors of one is equal to the	5020	5564
other and vice versa.	6232	6368
What are the two numbers in the	10744	10856
first pair? They are both under 300.	17926	18416
	9437056	9363584

WIND-UPS

Regular puzzle solvers may have noticed that from time to time we are influenced by one of our great puzzlist heroes, Charles Lutwidge Dodgson (Lewis Carroll). Throughout his life Carroll was fascinated with inventing and solving puzzles, and these are sprinkled throughout his popular works. Perhaps his most popular and lasting puzzle invention is 'Doublets', which you will know as the puzzle where the task is to change one word into another in several stages. Before you tackle this section, which includes an example of another of Carroll's favourite type of puzzle, 'Double Acrostic', we will leave you with one particular 'Doublet' puzzle, which remained unsolved by Mensa members until very recently, when several solutions were put forward. The puzzle is how to change 'MENSA' into 'WORLD' by altering just one letter each time. For the Mensa solution (seven stages) see A234. See if you can do it in less!

M E N S A

\- \- \- \- \-

\- \- \- \- \-

\- \- \- \- \-

\- \- \- \- \-

\- \- \- \- \-

\- \- \- \- \-

W O R L D

*194
Family Way

(See A185)

My two uncles and five cousins were all born on different days of
the week. Uncle Alan was born on a Friday and his daughters, my
cousins Judith and Mary, were born on a Monday and Saturday
respectively. My other uncle, Paul, was born on a Sunday and his
eldest son, my cousin Richard, was born on a Thursday. His other
sons, Roy and Terry, were born on the two remaining days of the
week; but which one was born on a Tuesday and which one was
born on a Wednesday?

*195
The Meeting

(See A230)

The man from the country at the top of the Himalayas came by
plane to meet the man from the Far East who was wearing a chain
round his neck. What was the weather when they met the man from
the Middle East?

(See A206)

Each couplet provides the clue to a word. When you have solved them, read down the first and last letters of the five words to reveal two further words.

> Very brief a note to play,
> Liquid measure either way.
>
> Here's a title I suspect,
> Turkey, Sir, yes with respect.
>
> Just an idea or a fancy,
> Opinion, belief or view you can see.
>
> Listen closely hear the clue,
> You paid attention, good for you!
>
> Now a line, or coalition,
> Revolve around it with precision.

(See A225)

Commence at the centre square and work from square to square horizontally, vertically and diagonally to find eight ships. Every square is used once only. Finish at the top right-hand square.

H	T	I	E	J	C	H	→
E	G	E	R	T	U	T	
R	Y	A	F	A	N	E	
H	C	N	✳	G	K	K	
T	A	K	O	I	R	R	
T	E	L	O	R	F	E	
R	S	P	T	A	W	L	

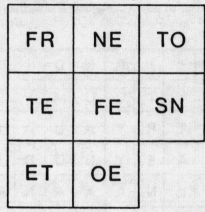

(See A148)

Find the missing square:

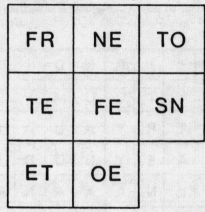

FR	NE	TO
TE	FE	SN
ET	OE	

Choose from:

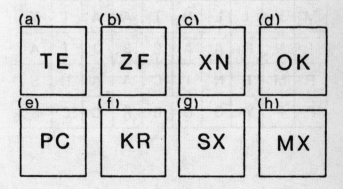

(a)	(b)	(c)	(d)
TE	ZF	XN	OK

(e)	(f)	(g)	(h)
PC	KR	SX	MX

(See A149)

Each horizontal and vertical line contains the jumbled letters of a country. Find the 20 countries. Every letter is used, but only once each.

A	A	I	I	R	N	D	I	I	G
R	N	I	I	U	U	M	P	I	E
K	A	T	R	Y	A	U	A	E	R
K	A	A	E	Y	N	U	D	E	O
T	A	L	N	A	A	A	N	M	O
L	R	A	E	I	G	R	N	A	I
M	Y	J	L	N	I	A	A	T	T
I	N	F	A	A	P	B	J	T	A
P	M	I	N	I	C	A	A	H	S
P	P	Y	G	U	B	R	C	C	S

Laughing Matter

(See A228)

We were determined that this section should have a happy ending, and if the sound of laughter isn't happy then we don't know what is. All these words are connected with humour.

(a)   – H – M – Y
(b)   – L – P – T – C –
(c)   – A – T – R
(d)   – A – I – A – U – E
(e)   – U – F – O – E – Y
(f)   – U – L – S – U –
(g)   – O – U – A – I – Y
(h)   – P – O –
(i)   – A – I – A – E
(j)   – A – I – E
(k)   – A – C –
(l)   – A – T – O –
(m)   – O – X
(n)   – O – E – Y

POTPOURRI

'It may well be doubted whether human ingenuity can construct an enigma of the kind which human ingenuity may not, by proper application resolve.'

Edgar Allan Poe

Consider the following list of words:

SEAT, LINE, FOOT, HOUSE.

Now choose one of the following words to add to the list:

TABLE, BED, CUPBOARD, WINDOW, FLOOR

(See A347)

What have the following in common?

A MINE

A HOLM OAK

A HUT

(See A305)

A man is walking his dog on the lead towards home at a steady 3 m.p.h. When they are 7 miles from home the man lets his dog off the lead. The dog immediately runs off towards home at 8 m.p.h. When the dog reaches the house it turns round and runs back to the man at the same speed. When it reaches the man it turns back for the house. This is repeated until the man gets home and lets in the dog. How many miles does the dog cover from being let off the lead to being let into the house?

(See A256)

A sultan tried to increase the number of women available for harems in his country by passing a law forbidding women to have another child once they gave birth to a son; as long as the children were girls they would be permitted to continue childbearing. 'Under this new law,' the sultan explained, 'you will see women having families such as four girls and one boy; ten girls and one boy; perhaps a solitary boy, and so on. This should obviously increase the ratio of women to men.'

Is this true?

(See A269)

Find 14 words of three or more letters contained in the grid.
Words run in any direction, backward and forward, horizontal,
vertical and diagonal, but only in a straight line.

Y	P	M	Y	L	S
S	R	H	X	Y	P
L	H	T	Z	M	Y
Y	S	Y	L	P	H
L	G	H	L	H	W
Y	H	R	R	Y	M

(See A281)

Which is the odd one out?

AIL

NOT

ROW

INCH

LOVER

THREAD

(See A283)

There is a single feature that these words have in common. What is it?

ENUMERATE

UNOCCUPIED

ONEROUS

UNUSUAL

BIRD

(See A352)

Shooting Match

Victor, Madsen and David each fired six shots, and each got 71 points. Victor's first two shots scored 22 points and Madsen's first shot scored only 3 points.

Who hit the bull's eye?

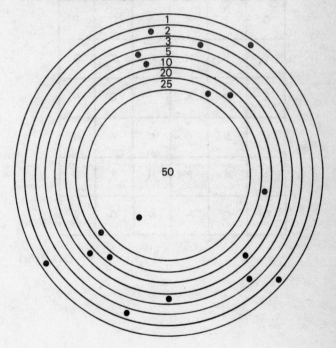

(See A241)

Divide the square into four identical sections. Each section must contain the same nine letters, which can be arranged into a nine-letter word.

O	P	C	N	C	P
C	Y	H	O	Y	O
C	P	A	C	O	N
H	N	O	C	A	H
A	Y	P	H	Y	O
O	C	A	N	O	C

(See A365)

To the purist a true anagram is a word or phrase the letters of which can be rearranged into another word or phrase which bears some relationship to the original. Our first puzzle in the section, Appropriate Anagrams, is a good illustration of this type of word play.

If you are a devotee of anagrams, you are in good company: Queen Victoria, for instance, was very fond of them. Here is one teaser which was said to have stumped her. Rearrange the letters 'ABONETY' into a seven-letter word (this may not be as easy as it at first appears). See how quickly you are able to come up with the correct solution (see A380).

All the solutions to the following have some relationship with the original.

1. They see (3, 4)
2. Truss neatly to be safe (6, 4, 4, 5)
3. Bear hit den (10)
4. I batch words (11)
5. Sear sad earth (6, 6)
6. Many a sad heart can whisper my prayer (1, 5, 9, 3, 1, 5, 3, 4)
7. HMS Pinafore (4, 3, 4)
8. I love Ms Nude (5, 2, 4)

(See A300)

Complete the words in each column, all of which end in 'E'. The scrambled letters in the section to the right of each column are an anagram of a word which will give you a clue to the word you are trying to find to put in the column.

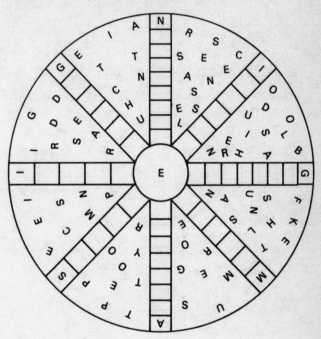

(See A255)

Complete the words in each column, all of which end in 'E'. The scrambled letters in the section to the right of each column are an anagram of a word which will give you a clue to the word you are trying to find to put in the column.

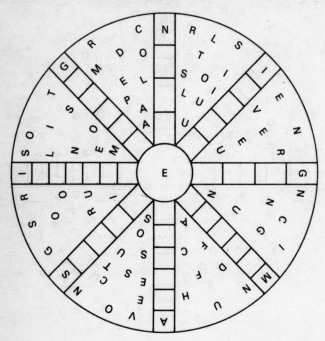

(See A259)

In each set below arrange the 14 words in pairs so that each pair is an anagram of another word or name. The seven words produced will have a linking theme. For example, if the words 'DIAL' and 'THAN' were in the list they could be paired to form an anagram of 'THAILAND', the theme being countries.

(a) BE
    COIN
    HE
    HOLD
    LAW
    NEAT
    PAD
    PIN
    RATE
    RAVE
    ROLE
    RUM
    TASK
    UPPER

(See A358)

(b) AGE
    FEAR
    GILD
    HAND
    MAID
    MAT
    MORE
    NO
    RAN
    RIG
    RUN
    SHOWING
    SON
    TAN

(See A319)

In each of the following unscramble the letters to find a word.
There are no two adjoining letters in the same shape.

(a) 13-letter word

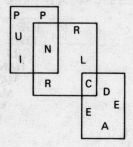

(See A296)

(b) 11-letter word

(See A350)

(c) 12-letter word

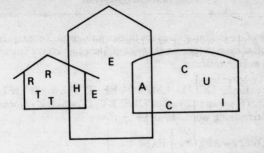

(See A332)

In each of the following study the three words given. Your task is to pair two of them to form an anagram of a word which is a synonym of the word remaining.

For example: DEED – EMPTY – REST. The words 'DEED' and 'REST' are an anagram of 'DESERTED', which is a synonym of the remaining word, 'EMPTY'.

1. OPEN – APRON – FAIR
2. WHEEL – SEER – OUT
3. CALL – MAIL – CROP
4. MAR – SEND – STINT
5. TAME – PEER – SOAK
6. MET – SOBER – REPEAT
7. LEG – MEEK – NET
8. CASE – LATE – DEED
9. GAIN – BEAD – WIT
10. SAND – DART – PAR
11. CUR – HEAD – MAIN
12. HOP – CUP – TRY
13. SMELL – LONE – CREED
14. SAD – PEACE – LARK

(See A270)

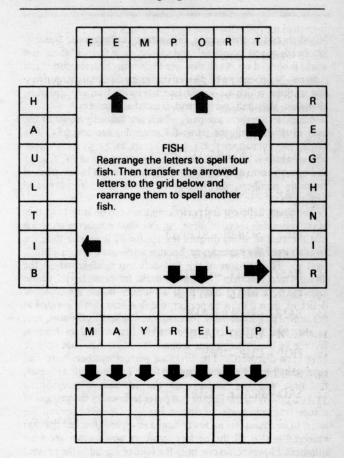

F E M P O R T

H A U L T I B

R E G H N I R

FISH
Rearrange the letters to spell four fish. Then transfer the arrowed letters to the grid below and rearrange them to spell another fish.

M A Y R E L P

(See A353)

MORE NUMBERS

Numbers can be challenging, fascinating, confusing and frustrating, but once you have developed an interest in them, a whole new world is opened up as you discover their many characteristics and patterns. Numbers can be divided into many different categories: a few of these which we would like to expound on are amicable, abundant, deficient, perfect and delectable numbers.

Amicable numbers are pairs which are mutually equal to the sum of all their aliquot parts: for example, 220 and 284. The aliquot parts of 220 are 1, 2, 4, 5, 10, 11, 20, 22, 44, 55 and 110, the sum of which is 284, while the aliquot parts of 284 are 1, 2, 4, 71 and 142, the sum of which is 220. There are seven known pairs of amicable numbers, the largest of which are 9,437,056 and 7,363,584.

Abundant, deficient and perfect numbers can be linked together as every number is one of these. An abundant number is one such that the sum of all its divisors (except itself) is greater than the number itself: for example, 12, because its divisors, 1, 2, 3, 4 and 6, total 16. The opposite of this is a deficient number, where the divisors total less than the number itself: for example, 10, whose divisors, 1, 2 and 5, total 8. If a number is not abundant or deficient, then it must be perfect, which means that it is equal to the sum of its aliquot parts: for example, 6, where its divisors, 1, 2, 3, also total 6. Perfect numbers were first named in Ancient Greece by the Pythagoreans around 500 BC and to date only 30 have been discovered. The first four perfect numbers were discovered before AD 100 and these are 6, 28, 496 and 8128. However, the next was not found until the fifteenth century; it is 33,550,336. With the help of computer technology the process of discovering new perfect numbers has been speeded up and the latest to be found has no fewer than 240 digits. One fact that has emerged is that all the perfect numbers now known are even numbers. However, no one from the time of Euclid to the present day has been able to prove that it is mathematically impossible for a perfect odd number to exist.

So, having dealt with amicable, abundant, deficient and perfect numbers, what, may you ask, is a delectable number? The answer is that a nine-digit number is delectable if (a) it contains the digits 1 to 9 exactly once each (no zero) and (b) the numbers created by taking the first *n* digits (*n* runs from 1 to 9) are each divisible by *n*, so the first digit is divisible by 1 (it always will be), the first two digits form a number divisible by 2, the first three digits form a number divisible by 3, and so on. It is known that there is one, and only one, number which meets the above conditions and can be called a delectable number. Can you find out what it is? (See A381.)

Insert the numbers 0 to 10 in the circles, so that for any particular circle the sum of the numbers in the circles connected directly to it equals the value corresponding to the number in that circle as given in the list below.

For example:

1 = 14 (4 + 7 + 3)
4 = 8 (7 + 1)
7 = 5 (4 + 1)
3 = 1

0 = 13
1 = 8
2 = 11
3 = 15
4 = 8
5 = 25
6 = 7
7 = 20
8 = 20
9 = 12
10 = 0

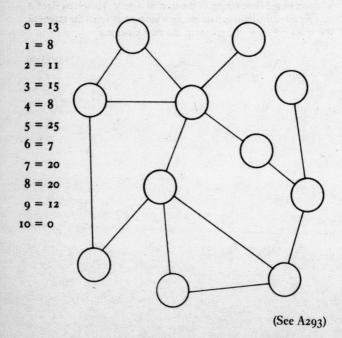

(See A293)

Average Speed

A car travels at a speed of 50 m.p.h. over a certain distance and then returns over the same distance at a speed of 30 m.p.h. What is the average speed for the total journey?

(See A327)

Train

A train travelling at a speed of 50 m.p.h. enters a tunnel which is 1½ miles long. The length of the train is ¼ mile. How long does it take for all of the train to pass through the tunnel, from the moment the front enters to the moment the rear emerges?

(See A339)

(a) Arrange the digits 1 to 9 once each only to form a single fraction that equals one eighth.

(See A276)

(b) Arrange the digits 1 to 9 once each only to form a single fraction that equals one seventh.

(See A243)

(c) Arrange the digits 1 to 9 once each only to form a single fraction that equals one sixth.

(See A340)

(d) Arrange the digits 1 to 9 once each only to form a single fraction that equals one half.

(See A248)

4.00 Everingham Maiden Stakes

1.	Anfield's Star	5–2
2.	Fresh from Victory	7–2
3.	James Star	9–2
4.	King of Sailors	5–1
5.	Lapiaffe	10–1
6.	Mariner's Law	16–1
7.	Turture	20–1
8.	Dayadari	?

What odds should the bookmaker give against Dayadari to give himself a 10 per cent margin on the race, assuming he balanced his books?

(See A260)

A lathe turner reduced the time taken to process a metal part from 35 minutes to 2½ minutes. He increased his cutting speed by 1690 inches per minute. To how much?

(See A252)

Three men, A, B and C, toss a coin in succession. The winner will be the first to throw a head. What are their respective chances?

(See A282)

How many times on average must an ordinary six-sided die be tossed before every number from 1 to 6 comes up at least once?

(See A240)

What is the missing number in this list?

1, 64, 125, 216, 729, 13824, 15625, ?, 132651

(See A320)

Square Numbers

Each horizontal and vertical line contains the digits of a four-figure square number. The digits are always in the right order, but not necessarily adjacent. Each digit is used once only, and they are all used. Find the 16 four-figure square numbers.

4	1	6	7	4	8	9	9
2	1	5	2	4	2	5	3
9	1	4	9	7	5	6	1
2	5	8	2	6	0	9	2
1	3	6	9	6	9	6	9
6	5	3	2	2	2	0	9
4	6	2	2	4	5	4	4
3	1	1	1	3	9	6	9

(See A376)

Cinderella has 89 buttons. There are six lots – 5–6–12–14–23–29 – each a different shade but only two colours – red and blue. The ugly sisters took away one lot, leaving twice as many reds as blues. Which lot was taken?

(See A279)

**228
Series

What is the missing number in this series?

1, 81, 2025, 3025, 9801, 88209, ?, 998001, 4941729

(See A264)

***229
Spot on the Table

A boy, recently home from school, wished to give his father an exhibition of his precocity. He pushed a large circular table into the corner of the room, so that it touched both walls, and he then pointed to a spot of ink on the extreme edge.

'Here is a little puzzle for you, pater,' said the youth. 'That spot is exactly 8 inches from one wall and 9 inches from the other. Can you tell me the diameter of the table without measuring it?'

The boy was overheard to tell a friend, 'It fairly beat the guv-'nor', but his father is known to have remarked to a City acquaintance that he solved the thing in his head in a minute. I often wonder which spoke the truth.

(See A342)

If 20 people, on parting, all shake hands with each other once, how many handshakes will there be altogether?

(See A298)

Select two positive integers at random, A + D, such that A < D. Select two more positive integers at random, B + C, such that A < B < C < D.

For example: 68 – 187 – 1667 – 2095

Are the chances that B + C = an odd number:

50 per cent?

less than 50 per cent?

more than 50 per cent?

(See A242)

Find the smallest possible number which when multiplied by 29 looks the same as it did before, but with the addition of the same digit on each end.

For example: ABC × 29 = YABCY

(See A273)

WORD PLAY

It is often said that to have a mastery of words is to have in one's possession the ability to produce order out of chaos and that command of vocabulary is a true measure of intelligence. As such, vocabulary tests are widely used in intelligence testing.

Here are a few examples of word play for you to try before tackling the rest of our word puzzles in this section (for the answers see A382).

Find in the English language:

1. A word which, without a change in pronunciation, has two directly contrary meanings;

2. A seven-letter word which contains each of the five vowels once;

3. An 11-letter word whose odd letters spell out a word and whose even letters spell out a word;

4. A nine-letter word which is an anagram of a state of the USA;

5. The only word to have the letters 'UFA' embedded in it;

6. A word having five consecutive vowels embedded in it;

7. Two words which are synonyms when used as verbs but antonyms when used as adjectives, adverbs or nouns;

Using the following letters only, fill in the pyramid so that each horizontal line forms a word. Use each letter as many times as necessary. Each word formed must consist of the same letters as the word above it, in any order, plus one additional letter.

A, E, L, N, R, S, T

nine-letter word base

(See A333)

Something in Common

What do the following words have in common?

HONOUR
CHEQUE
THEATRE
LICENCE
CENTRE

(See A331)

Alphabet

Use the 26 letters of the alphabet once each to complete these
words.

ABCDEFGHIJKLM
NOPQRSTUVWXYZ

1. D – – –   6. – A –

2. – O – E   7. – U A – –

3. – A L – R –   8. – O –

4. H A – E   9. – A – – A

5. – U – – A –   10. – O – –

(See A325)

Spiral clockwise round the perimeter and finish at the centre square to spell out the nine-letter words. Each word commences at one of the four corner squares.

A		C
	E	A
I	T	

* (a) (See A249)

	U	
S	E	T
O		A

** (b) (See A322)

	G	
I	D	I
K	E	

* (c) (See A330)

B		S
E	R	
	N	A

* (d) (See A274)

R		U
U	E	O
	S	

** (e) (See A251)

In each of the following spell out the 15-letter word by going through the labyrinth one room at a time. Go into each room once only. You may go into the corridor as many times as you wish.

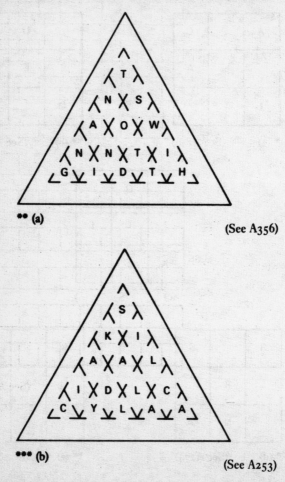

** (a)

(See A356)

*** (b)

(See A253)

Use all the 30 small words scattered below once each only to construct 10 words (three small words per word).

DANCE

FACT

DAM   ONE

   EGO

HER   MALE

   LOP   HE

TO   ABLE

     HABIT

   RISE

WOE   FAT

     CAT

FEAT   IN

   EVE   HER

OR

     RED

   ANT

     LESS

AGE

   AT

GET   BEG

   TEN

     RED

(See A375)

229

Fill in the spaces to find the words. All letters are in the correct order and the overlapping letter appears twice. The word might appear reading clockwise or anticlockwise.

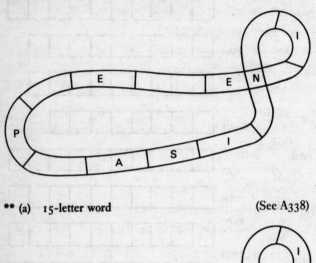

** (a) 15-letter word (See A338)

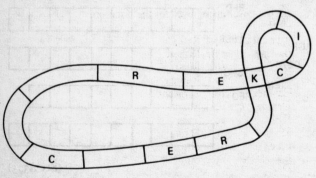

** (b) 14-letter word (See A292)

Each clue is solved by joining together two words from the 25 listed. You will use 24 words. Find the odd word left over.

A.   Does this recluse use a gin in his grounds?

B.   Thigh-slapping transvestite.

C.   In charge of the road works.

D.   12 makeshift people who are biased.

E.   Does this marauder of the deep like the sun?

F.   Charge for the cutlery and get the bird.

G.   Difficult to get Jackson out unless the bowler is Hadrian.

H.   Hire the knight, the price looks good.

I.   This bird will do well in the marathon.

J.   Sounds like an irritable monster.

K.   Russian sea-faring lepidopterist.

L.   Put the government away for the duration.

1.	Admiral	14.	Red
2.	Basking	15.	Rigged
3.	Bill	16.	Road
4.	Boy	17.	Runner
5.	Cabinet	18.	Sergeant
6.	Dragon	19.	Shark
7.	Drill	20.	Snap
8.	Filing	21.	Spoon
9.	Free	22.	Squash
10.	Jury	23.	Stone
11.	Lance	24.	Trappist
12.	Monk	25.	Wall
13.	Principal		

(See A272)

Cryptic Elimination 2

Each clue is solved by joining together two words from the 25 listed. You will use 24 words. Find the odd word left over.

A. A bird for the winter season.

B. A simple movement in dancing.

C. Furry creature with a ringer? No, it's a plant.

D. You would expect to see the bird flying.

E. This mammal could mean murder.

F. Starting point for a race on board ship.

G. Hat worn when hunting animals.

H. Stuck up! Should try eating sweets properly.

I. Opposite of open-handed.

J. It may bounce in the post office.

K. Rapid writing system for 5-foot worker.

L. Female advertising executive in orbit.

1.	Bell	
2.	Deer	
3.	Fisted	
4.	Goose	
5.	Hand	
6.	Hare	
7.	Jay	
8.	Killer	
9.	Line	
10.	Nosed	
11.	Plimsoll	
12.	Rubber	
13.	Short	
14.	Side	
15.	Silver	
16.	Snow	
17.	Space	
18.	Stalker	
19.	Stamp	
20.	Step	
21.	Tight	
22.	Toffee	
23.	Walking	
24.	Whale	
25.	Woman	

(See A258)

Place a four-letter word in the centre so that when added on to the end of the first four-letter word it will produce an eight-letter word, and when placed in front of the second four-letter word it will produce another eight-letter word.

1.	WORM	– – – –	AWAY
2.	FOLK	– – – –	BIRD
3.	BACK	– – – –	ROOM
4.	CLUB	– – – –	BALL
5.	TURN	– – – –	LAND
6.	FORE	– – – –	PLAY
7.	DOWN	– – – –	SIDE
8.	WOOD	– – – –	MILL
9.	GOLD	– – – –	HOUR
10.	TYPE	– – – –	LIFT

(See A355)

Here are two lists of words. Each word in List A has two possible pair words in List B. Each word in List B has two possible pair words in List A. There are two possible solutions. Pair a word from each list until you have eight pairs.

List A		*List B*	
NUPTIALS	MAIDEN	RING	WEDDING
SOLE	TOREADOR	HORSE	MATADOR
BULL	SEA	SEVILLE	LEMON
DIAMOND	ORANGE	SWORDFISH	NUBILE

(See A250)

In the example a circle of three six-letter words – oncost, stripe and person – each overlap by two letters. Each word is divided into two-letter groups and these two-letter groups from the circle are arranged in alphabetical order, that is, CO, ON, PE, RI, RS, ST.

Now try to unscramble the following to find a circle of eight six-letter words, each word overlapping its neighbour by two letters.

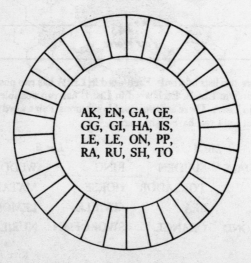

AK, EN, GA, GE,
GG, GI, HA, IS,
LE, LE, ON, PP,
RA, RU, SH, TO

(See A343)

Fit the words into the six spaces around each black centre, either clockwise or anticlockwise, so that all the words link up.

TYPING	BOVINE	PANDER
GROVES	GINGER	NINETY
SEVENS	PASSES	SPACES
SEDANS	COBALT	LANDED

(See A261)

Find seven words each commencing with the central letter 'K'.
Words are in adjacent squares in any direction and each letter is
used once only.

```
O   O   S   L   T   B   U

A   R   S   E   T   B   T

G   N   A   E   I   N   Z

E   R   !   K   I   K   A

H   N   O   A   I   O   J

S   G   L   R   E   B   U

I   F   N   I   Z   T   I
```

(See A299)

DIAGRAMS

The puzzles here are not tests of numeracy or literacy but concern diagrammatic representation. Widely used in intelligence testing, diagrammatic tests are considered to be culture-fair and test raw intelligence without the influence of prior knowledge. They will probe your understanding of space relationships, pattern and design. At first some of these puzzles may appear daunting, but our advice is to stick at them, because after careful study the solution may suddenly appear to you. As with all the puzzles in this book, please do not rush to look up the answer if you cannot see a solution immediately. Remember that a puzzle which baffles you initially may suddenly seem soluble if you take a fresh look some time later. Puzzles, to a great extent, are like problems in life: they often need to be worked at and thought about before the reward of a successful solution is obtained.

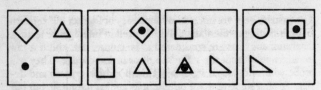

Which of the following continues the above sequence?

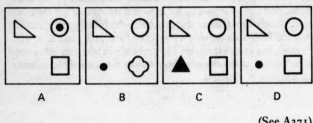

A   B   C   D

(See A371)

*248
Odd One Out

Which of the following is the odd one out?

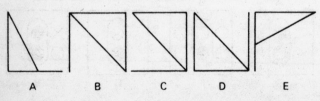

A   B   C   D   E

(See A247)

Look along each line horizontally and then down each line vertically to find what, logically, should be in the missing square.

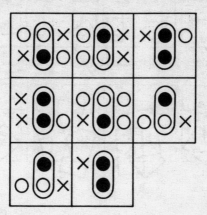

Choose from:

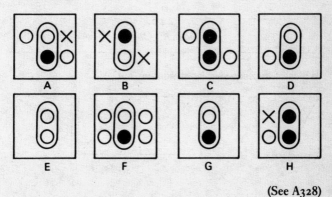

(See A328)

Study the three rectangles below. Which one of the options given has the most in common with them?

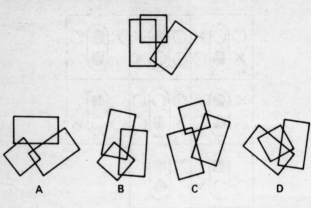

A   B   C   D

(See A317)

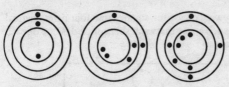

Which of the following continues the above sequence?

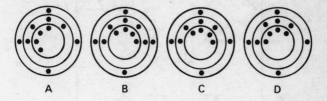

A   B   C   D

(See A275)

In both of the following divide the squares into four parts of equal size and shape in such a way that each shape includes one of each of the four symbols.

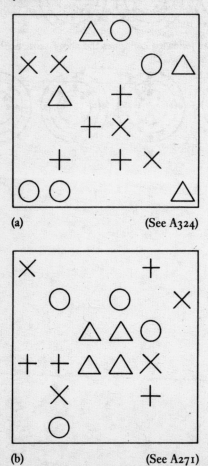

(a)   (See A324)

(b)   (See A271)

For us one of the joys in compiling puzzles is to root out good quotations, and you will find several sprinkled throughout this book. We find that quotations can be thought-provoking, appropriate and amusing and we hope that you will share our enjoyment of them.

Start at the letter 'T' in the bottom right-hand corner and by Knight's moves* spell out a quotation by Blaise Pascal.

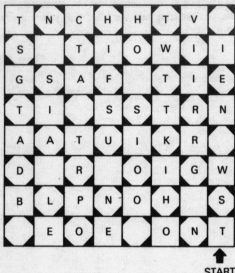

START

* In chess the knight is the only piece allowed to jump over other pieces. It can move one square horizontally and two vertically or two horizontally and one vertically (as in the diagram to the right). Usually represented by a horse's head, it is occasionally referred to as the horse (as in the Arabic version).

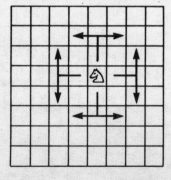

(See A244)

'Let's get out of these wet clothes and into a dry martini.'

Using all 45 letters of the above quotation by Robert Benchley, complete the pyramid. Across clues are given, but in no particular order.

CLUES:

Travel

Avoided deliberately

Neuter pronoun of the third person

Military pageant

In good health

Fireproof cooking dish

Pronoun of the first person singular

Short sacred vocal composition

Indifferent dullness

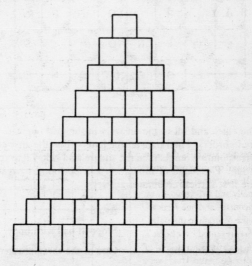

(See A357)

The grid contains a quotation by Francis Bacon. The letters in the columns go into the squares above. You have to select which squares.

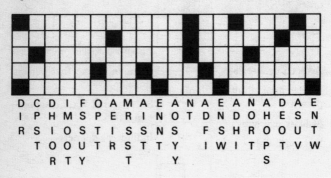

D	C	D	I	F	O	A	M	A	E	A	N	A	E	A	N	A	D	A	E
I	P	H	M	S	P	E	R	I	N	O	T	D	N	D	O	H	E	S	N
R	S	I	O	S	T	I	S	S	N	S		F	S	H	R	O	O	U	T
	T	O	O	U	T	R	S	T	T	Y			I	W	I	T	P	T	V	W
	R	T	Y		T				Y						S				

(See A301)

Solve the clues and fill in the answers in the grid opposite (the clues are in order). Then transfer the letters from the answers to their corresponding numbers in the square grid below it to reveal a quotation. The name of the author can be found by reading down the first vertical column of answers.

CLUES:

Cogitate	Avoid
Take a piece at draughts	Stopped ball with body
Shaft of wood with broad blade	One of the three musketeers
Nutritious seed	Deep narrow gorge
Power	One or other of two
	Move tail vigorously

(See A295)

Magic number squares have intrigued mathematicians and puzzle fanatics for centuries. The first example here dates from around the beginning of the 10th century AD and is part of the Chinese Loh River scroll. Perfect magic squares must use consecutive numbers, each one only once, to produce the same total across each horizontal line, down each vertical line and from corner to corner. Not only does The Loh River 15 achieve this but, by using beads instead of written numbers, the compiler of nearly 1000 years ago has brilliantly added an additional dimension to the puzzle by showing even numbers as black and odd numbers as white.

Over the years magic squares have acquired a reputation for occult and mystical properties and have been inscribed on charms to ward off evil spirits and bring good luck. The real charm of these squares, however, is the seemingly endless mathematical properties which they reveal and the number of different ways which they can be constructed. We have illustrated this in Q257 – our five 5 × 5 magic squares puzzle.

During the seventeenth century, French mathematicians

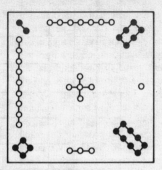

1. The Loh River 15

52	61	4	13	20	29	36	45
14	3	62	51	46	35	30	19
53	60	5	12	21	28	37	44
11	6	59	54	43	38	27	22
55	58	7	10	23	26	39	42
9	8	57	56	41	40	25	24
50	63	2	15	18	31	34	47
16	1	64	49	48	33	32	17

2. The Franklin 260

took the construction of magic squares further, and later, in the eighteenth century, the American diplomat, scientist and author Benjamin Franklin became one of the world's leading authorities on magic squares (possibly as a result of his years spent as a diplomat in Paris) and devised new types of squares with intriguing patterns. In the second example here, devised by Franklin, all horizontal and vertical lines total 260, but alas, to purists it cannot be classed as a true magic square as the sums of the two corner-to-corner lines do not equal this total. However, more importantly, this square does introduce us to what is known as the property of bent diagonals and symmetrical patterns which produce the same magic total of 260. We leave you to discover as many of these patterns as you can (turn to A278 when you think you have exhausted all possibilities).

A century after Franklin, in England, another magic square guru, Dr Frierson, was able to improve The Franklin 260 by devising the mind-blowing square in the third example. Not only do all horizontal, vertical and corner-to-corner lines total 260, as demanded by the purists, but again there are many symmetrical patterns for you to discover (see A329). In addition, there is a further startling property whereby the whole divides into four 4 × 4 magic squares, each adding up to 130.

Before leaving you to tackle the kaleidoscope of magic square puzzles which follows, here are a few hints which will enable you to construct at least one magic square for every odd number from 3 × 3 upwards.

64	57	4	5	56	49	12	13
3	6	63	58	11	14	55	50
61	60	1	8	53	52	9	16
2	7	62	59	10	15	54	51
48	41	20	21	40	33	28	29
19	22	47	42	27	30	39	34
45	44	17	24	37	36	25	32
18	23	46	43	26	31	38	35

3. The Frierson 260

30	39	48	1	10	19	28
38	47	7	9	18	27	29
46	6	8	17	26	35	37
5	14	16	25	34	36	45
13	15	24	33	42	44	4
21	23	32	41	43	3	12
22	31	40	49	2	11	20

4. The 7 × 7 Standard 175

Taking, for example, the 7 × 7 square shown in the fourth example, the system of construction holds good for any odd number. It is simply to start at the middle square of the top row and move diagonally upwards (imagine four squares reproduced adjacent to the sides of the main square and move into them; the numbers reappear in the same position in the main square – see the fifth example on p. 250).

When you reach the top of a line, you go to the bottom of the next line to the right: for example, from 1 to 2. When you reach the end of a line, you go to the beginning of the line above; for example, from 45 to 46. When you reach the top right-hand-corner square, you go to the square below: for example, from 28 to 29. The only other move is when your upward diagonal path is blocked by another number, in which case you go to the square directly below: for example, from 35 to 36.

Easy when you know how!

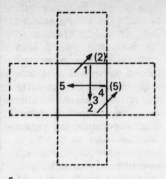

5.

It is possible to arrange the numbers 1 to 25 in several ways to form a magic square where each horizontal, vertical and corner-to-corner line totals 65. Can you insert the numbers 1 to 25 in each of the grids below to find five different 5 × 5 magic squares? In each square two of the numbers are already positioned and your task is to insert the remaining numbers correctly.

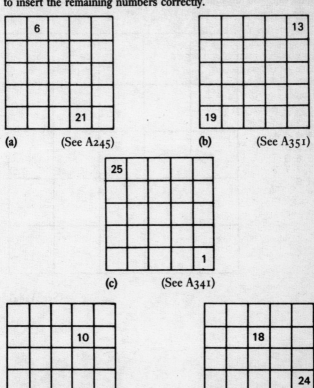

(a)   (See A245)

(b)   (See A351)

(c)   (See A341)

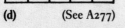

(d)   (See A277)

(e)   (See A306)

When the sum of the digits of a number will divide exactly by nine, then the number itself will also divide by nine: for example, 2673 and 2 + 6 + 7 + 3 = 18. With this in mind, place the digits into the grid so that each horizontal, vertical and corner-to-corner line, when read both forwards and backwards, will divide exactly by nine, and also the sum of the four corner numbers will divide by nine.

1, 1, 1
2, 2, 2
3, 3
4, 4, 4, 4
5, 5, 5
6, 6, 6
7, 7, 7, 7
8, 8
9

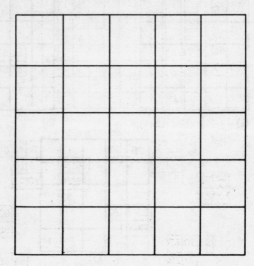

(See A284)

Insert the sections into the grid to form a 10 × 10 magic square so that each horizontal, vertical and corner-to-corner line totals 505.

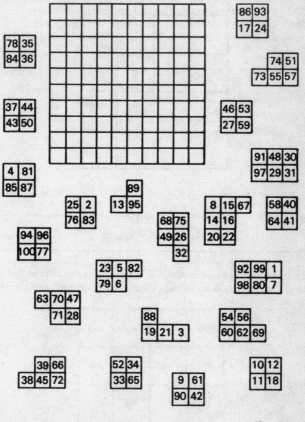

(See A257)

Fill the grid with the numbers 1 to 16 to form a magic square so that each horizontal, vertical and corner-to-corner line totals 34. One number is already inserted.

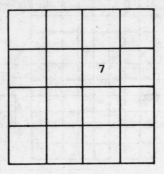

(See A361)

—— **261** ——
The Incredible Square!

Here is a magic square in which all horizontal, vertical and corner-to-corner lines add up to 264. What is most unusual about it?

96	11	89	68
88	69	91	16
61	86	18	99
19	98	66	81

(See A280)

Arrange the numbers 1 to 19 so that all 15 connected straight lines
(that is, horizontals and diagonals) add up to the same total.

For example: A + B + C = B + E + I + M

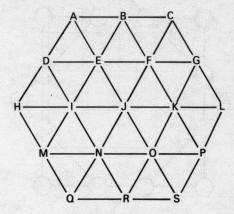

(See A377)

Distribute the numbers 1 to 16 around the nodes so that each of the eight lines adds up to the same number.

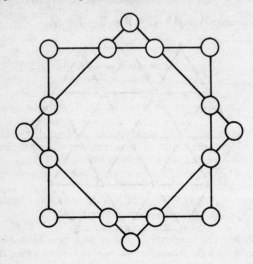

(See A294)

Kickself puzzles, the ones which usually have an 'obvious when you know it' answer, are well known in Mensa circles. Here are some typical examples. What was the first human artefact to break the sound barrier? (A304). Why are round manhole covers safer than square manhole covers? (A310). On a building site some workmen tell their foreman they have just found a coin marked 10 BC; why does the foreman suddenly realize they must be pulling his leg? (A314). Why are 1989 50p coins worth more than 1988 50p coins? (A326). A woman has borne just two sons, which she gave birth to on the same day at 30-minute intervals; they are identical, but not twins. What is the explanation? (A364).

Each month a kickself puzzle appears in *Mensa*, the journal of British Mensa, with a prize for the first correct solution drawn out. We are usually inundated with correct entries but occasionally one puzzle appears which seems, for whatever reason, to stump almost everyone. Before leaving you to tackle our following compilation of kickself puzzles, here is one which was solved by only a handful of people when it appeared in *Mensa* in April 1987.

In Oxford Street, London, I saw one of these new-fangled buses. One cannot tell the front from the rear and, when stationary, in which direction the bus is heading. Which way is the bus heading: A or B?

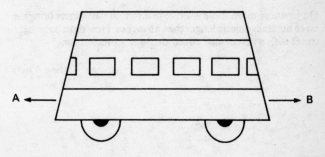

(See A378)

*264
Signpost

A traveller in a strange country, with no map, comes to a crossroads where a signpost has been knocked down. How can he find his way without asking anyone for directions?

(See A246)

**265
Unique Number

What is unique about the number 854917632?

(See A379)

**266
Ceremonial Sword

On Japanese trains there is a rule that forbids passengers bringing on to the train objects longer than 36 inches. How did a passenger travel with a ceremonial sword that was 42 inches long?

(See A288)

A Greek was born on the 26th day of 20 BC and died on the 26th day of AD 60. How many years did he live?

(See A344)

In Manhattan the avenues run north to south and the streets run east to west. 11 friends who work at the intersection of the roads marked with an * wish to meet on a street corner with the least possible amount of total walking distance. On which corner should they meet?

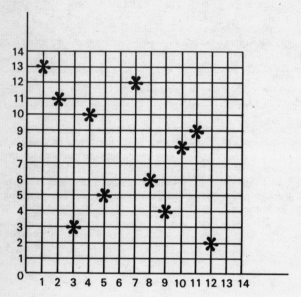

(See A254)

A full cask of wine has a bung hole on the top surface. You have only a bottle full of water. Without moving the cask or damaging it, and using no other appliances, how can you obtain a bottle of wine from the cask?

(See A370)

The driver and his pantechnicon weigh 10 tons. His cargo of 200 uncaged sleeping pigeons weighs 200 lb. The driver approaches a 10-ton-limit bridge, stops, gets out, bangs on the side of the pantechnicon to make the pigeons fly about, gets back in and drives over the bridge safely. In practice his actions were correct because he managed to cross the bridge safely, but was his reasoning correct in theory?

(See A291)

An Arab came to the riverside,
With a donkey bearing an obelisk,
But he did not venture to ford the tide,
For he had too good an *.

* What is the missing word?

(See A303)

Can you draw the next figure in this series?

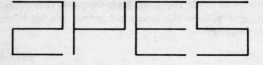

(See A268)

Every member of the Luncheon Club is either a truther, who always tells the truth when asked a question, or a liar, who always answers with a lie. When I visited the club for the first time, I found its members, all men, seated around a large circular table, having lunch. There was no way to distinguish truthers from liars by their appearance and so I asked each man in turn which he was. This proved unenlightening. Each man naturally assured me he was a truther. I tried again, this time asking each man whether his neighbour on the left was a truther or a liar. To my surprise each told me the man on his left was a liar. Later in the day, back home and typing up my notes on the luncheon, I discovered I had forgotten to record the number of men at the table. I telephoned the club's president. He told me the number was 37. After hanging up I realized that I could not be sure of this figure because I did not know whether the president was a truther or a liar. I then telephoned the club's secretary.

'No, no,' the secretary said. 'Our president, unfortunately, is an unmitigated liar. There were actually 40 men at the table.'

Which man, if either, should I believe? Suddenly I saw a simple way to resolve the matter.

Was it 37 or 40?

(See A349)

Nothing seems to grip the public's imagination more than a treasure hunt. The Klondike Gold Rush of 1896 in America was a prime example and also, more recently in England, there was the occasion when an author buried some treasure and then published a book giving cryptic clues to its location and people enthusiastically combed the countryside for days looking for it. Incidentally, the treasure was never found.

Since 1845, in America, many people have devoted a great deal of their time to trying to break what is known as the Beale Cyphers in an attempt to find the whereabouts of several tons of gold, silver and jewels supposedly buried near the town of Montvale (formally Bufords), Virginia. It was a Virginian, Thomas J. Beale, who set out with a party of men in 1817 on a hunting trip which eventually took them towards the Colorado mountains. Here they discovered gold and stayed on to mine both gold and silver for 18 months. Then in November 1819, fearing for their safety and their vast fortune, they returned to Virginia to hide their treasure in a secret excavation six feet below ground. Two years later they again returned to the site with some $13,000 in jewels, which they had purchased in St Louis. During this time Tom Beale had become acquainted with Robert Morriss, the proprietor of a hotel where he stayed, and he entrusted to Morriss a strong iron box for safekeeping. Later he wrote to Morriss, asking him to keep the box for 10 years and telling him that if he had not by then called to collect it, to open it up. Beale was never heard of again, but to be on the safe side Morriss waited for almost 25 years before finally opening the box in 1845. Inside he found several sheets of paper and letters telling the story of the treasure, together with three cryptograms, or ciphers, giving details of the location of the treasure, its contents and Beale's next of kin. One letter promised that the three ciphers could easily be cracked using a key which would be sent to Morriss, but it never arrived. As Morriss could not crack the ciphers he enlisted the help of a friend, who became obsessed with them and after some 20 years was finally able to crack one of the ciphers, the one giving the contents of the vault of treasure.

The method which he discovered Beale had used was to take the Declaration of Independence and allocate each word a number, from WHEN = 1 to HONOR = 1322, then, taking the first letter of the word which corresponded to each number of the cipher, the message was spelt out, starting: 115(I), 73(H), 24(A), 807(V), 37(E), 52(D), 49(E), 17(P), 31(O), 62(S), 647(I), 22(T) ...

Since then, the remaining two ciphers have remained a mystery, despite many thousands of hours of research and effort, and no treasure has been found. Whether the Beale treasure is genuine or a hoax we cannot be sure, but research is still continued, especially by the members of the Beale Cypher Association in Pennsylvania.

No story could better illustrate the appeal of codes and ciphers. The handful of puzzles which follows contains some original codes and ciphers of our own invention. We cannot promise you any buried treasure, but hopefully you will spend some entertaining minutes or hours solving them, and for any that you cannot crack, at least you will not have to wait years for the answer, as all you have to do is turn to the back of the book!

Decode the following:

686, 323, 311, 457, 010, 819, 001, 121, 663, 879, 324, 775, 100, 030, 777, 446, 185, 441, 239, 151, 011, 212, 010, 784, 488

(See A366)

***275
Coded Message

Decode the following to reveal a message:

ECHO, MOOD, LIMA, SIERRA, SOUND, PAPA, BEACH, TANGO, IDEA, WHISKY, SCREEN, QUEEN, ROMEO, MAE, WEST, CROON, CHAMPAGNE, QUEST, WROTE, FOIL, IMMORTAL, FIELDS.

(See A302)

Each cryptogram is a straight substitution code where every letter
of the alphabet has been replaced by another. Each of the three is
in a different code.

1. OE XYHSWSNH SN O WOE BRX NHOJHN O
   MJXNNBXJZ YPFFCD BSHR O IXPEHOSE YDE.

   (See A307)

2. XNW YOH ENG DYPFWD ENWH XNPHZD ZG
   ETGHZ NOD XNGMZNX GA DGYWGHW NW SOH
   KFOYW PX GH.

   – BGHWD' FOE

   (See A372)

3. VT FHTHYUN, BAH UYB JQ FJXHYTDHTB
   IJTRVRBR VT BUCVTF UR DKIA DJTHO UR
   ZJRRVLNH QYJD JTH ZUYBO JQ BAH IVBVPHTR BJ
   FVXH BJ BAH JBAHY.

   – XJNBUVYH

   (See A289)

Decode the following:

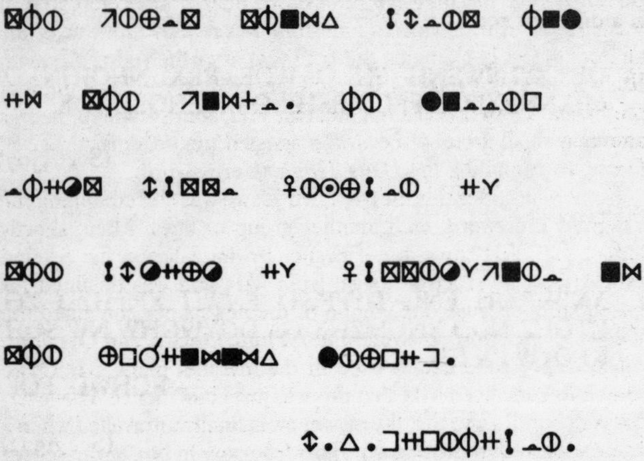

(See A346)

1988 was not only the year in which the 75th anniversary of the publication of the first-ever crossword puzzle was celebrated; it was also the year in which a milestone was reached for one of the authors of this book, being the 50th year after the young Kenneth Russell began his interest in compiling crosswords. As a pupil of the Strand Grammar School in Tulse Hill, south London, he was among a small group of boys who assisted the headmaster, L. S. Dawe, in compiling the *Daily Telegraph* crossword.

Some years after this, in 1945, Mr Dawe was still compiling the *Telegraph* crossword, with another group of boys, when, shortly before the D-day invasion of France by the Allies in the Second World War, he received a visit from MI5 and was detained for questioning because one edition of the newspaper contained the following crossword answers: Fido, Pluto, Omaha and Overlord. All were key code names used in the invasion plans. Mr Dawe somehow convinced MI5 that this was just coincidence. However, it was not until 1980 that the mystery was finally unravelled when a letter appeared in the *Sunday Times* from an old boy of the school who had been a member of the crossword team. He confessed to having been the culprit. It appeared that his mother had been evacuated to Lincolnshire during the war and had found work in an American Air Force base. He frequently visited her at weekends and moved freely about the camp, where these secret code names were often bandied about. The names had stuck with him and he had, as a result, fed them into the crossword grid.

Ken's interest in crosswords has never waned since those traumatic times of half a century ago, and together we have devised the following selection of variations on the traditional crossword theme. We start with our tribute to the world's first-ever cruciverbalist (crossword constructor), Liverpool-born Arthur Wynne, whom we have to thank for his invention of 79 years ago.

The grid below is the exact design used by Arthur Wynne when he compiled the first crossword puzzle, which appeared in the *New York World* on Sunday 21 December 1913. Called a word-cross puzzle, it is reproduced here with a completely new set of clues and answers.

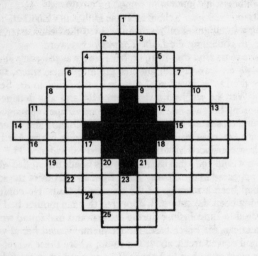

CLUES:

Across

2. Piece of timber (3)
4. Passageway in theatre (5)
6. Seriously thoughtful (7)
8. Type of footwear (4)
9. Waist band (4)
11. Mild expletive (4)
12. Want (4)
14. Garrison (4)
15. Grasp (4)
16. Hard work (4)
18. Hard grating noise (4)
19. Christmas (4)
21. Eat dinner (4)
22. Closest at hand (7)
24. Rap sharply (5)
25. Large deer (3)

Down

1. Low tufted plant (4)
2. Fabric with raised nap (4)
3. Fluently insincere (4)
4. Long period of time (4)
5. Not odd (4)
6. Part of a whole (7)
7. Dignified and graceful (7)
8. Member of nobility (5)
10. Neatly brief and concise (5)
11. Small round mark (3)
13. Plunge (3)
17. National emblem of Wales (4)
18. Expose to danger (4)
20. Narrow road (4)
21. Ship's platform (4)
23. Turn over and over (4)

(See A313)

Place the 3 × 3 sets in the grid to complete the crossword.

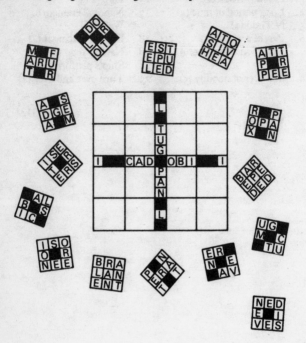

(See A316)

Insert the 26 letters of the alphabet into the grid, using each one only once, to form a crossword. The clues are in no particular order.

CLUES:

Defensive players

Trot along

Behind the true time

The west wind

Exasperate

Express amount of

Indistinct

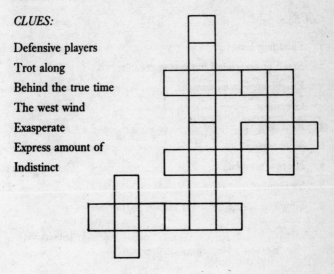

(See A265)

The answers to the clues are to be found in the grid in letter order. They are all nine-letter words. For example: Deciduous.

CLUES:

1. Shedding leaves
2. Small underground burrowing creature
3. Exaggerated statement
4. Greatness
5. Reclining
6. Trite saying
7. Narrow-minded
8. Sweetmeat
9. Simple covering for lower middle part of body

(See A285)

H	L	R	L	D	H	E	W	M
E	O	Y	E	I	I	A	A	I
D	I	G	R	T	C	Q	P	C
I	N	T	N	T	E	U	U	E
I	B	C	H	I	M	O	R	D
C	U	B	T	B	L	W	R	O
O	E	O	O	I	O	U	I	U
L	T	U	S	N	D	N	R	C
H	E	S	M	M	T	E	D	E

'A' Frame

Each horizontal and vertical line indicates the consonants of a word which can be completed by adding a number of 'A' vowels. The two-figure number at the end of each line indicates the number of consonants and 'A' vowels: for example, 3–2 indicates three consonants and two 'A' vowels. Each letter in the grid is used once only and all letters must be used. The consonants to be used in each line are not necessarily in the correct order or adjacent.

CLUES:

Across
1. Trite
2. Hoax
3. Danger
4. Eastern native
5. Coward
6. Gather
7. Indian sailor

Down
1. Pineapple
2. Chasm
3. Certain
4. Waterway
5. Structures
6. White ball in bowls
7. Parrot

(See A262)

	1	2	3	4	5	6	7	
1	L	S	T	B	S	N	W	3-2
2	S	N	R	N	C	J	D	4-2
3	H	S	Z	L	D	R	C	4-2
4	B	Y	D	C	W	K	R	2-2
5	T	B	D	D	L	S	R	5-2
6	N	M	N	S	L	S	M	3-2
7	N	L	M	C	R	C	S	4-2
	3-3	4-1	4-3	3-2	4-1	3-1	3-2	

There was a crooked man who walked a crooked mile. He found some crooked silver pieces which had fallen out of the crooked pocket of a crooked man in charge of a crooked football match by a crooked stile. With the crooked money he bought crooked mice and a crooked snake and they all lived together with twin girls in a crooked house and he puts up with the racket which sounds louder each day.

Find the eight clues, solve them and place the answers in the grid.

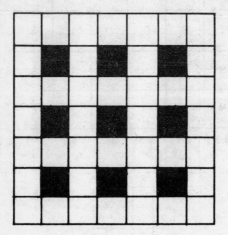

(See A334)

Each number has a choice of possible letters, as shown in the key.
Select the correct letter for each square to form eight seven-letter
interlocking words.

1	1	6	2	2	6	7
5	■	2	■	5	■	9
5	1	7	3	8	2	7
3	■	3	■	3	■	7
2	5	6	3	5	5	2
2	■	2	■	7	■	5
6	2	7	3	7	7	7

KEY:

1	A	B	C
2	D	E	F
3	G	H	I
4	J	K	L
5	M	N	O
6	P	Q	R
7	S	T	U
8	V	W	X
9	Y	Z	

(See A368)

Place all the words below into the two empty grids to form two crossword puzzles.

NO	TAP	EON	RED	BETS	TOOL
ME	SPA	NIT	APT	ACHE	ERAS
IT	SHY	ANT	YET	EVEN	EMIT
SO	LAP	ROE	ACE	WETS	SLIP
TO	PUT	LAM	MOW	KNOW	SLAP
IN	SON	TEA	TOW	AIDE	SICK
AS	BIT	HEN	SAT	PETS	EDGY
IS	TEG	GET	ART	SPEW	TOIL

MOTET	DRAUGHT	APPEALING
NOTES	EPAULET	PRESCRIBE
SEDAN		CRINOLINE
SPENT		IMPRUDENT

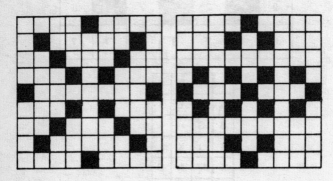

(See A318)

Insert the 26 letters of the alphabet to complete the crossword.

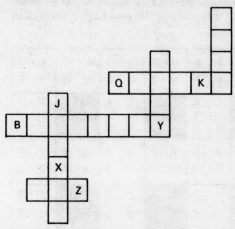

Seven of the letters have already been inserted.

A ⒷB C D E F G
H I Ⓙ Ⓚ L M N
O P Ⓠ R S T U
V W Ⓧ Ⓨ Ⓩ

(See A309)

Clueless Crossword

In each square there are four letters. Your task is to cross out three of each four, leaving one letter in each square, so that the crossword is made up in the usual way with good English interlocking words.

T A / E C	X O / R A	S N / E P		D A / N C	A Q / E B	A R / D O	F D / Y T
A B / R O	███	I A / R H	███	X A / V U	███	A H / R I
E W / A O	E V / G J	Z E / I T	A E / R P	U A / I T	G I / A N	Y N / E G
I M / L S	███	F D / O C	███	T E / D U	███	E A / H R
O E / P J	X R / C B	L N / F E	I E / T L	Q E / T L	M X / U B	N T / E D

(See A286)

In this section we present a diverse collection of puzzles which have just one thing in common – their high degree of difficulty.

The plumber left the taps running in the bath with the plug out. The hot water tap on would fill the bath in 54 seconds. The cold water tap on would fill the bath in 48 seconds. The plug out would release a bath full of water in 30 seconds. Would the bath ever fill up?

(See A362)

The addition sum below is written out in a very unusual way. Try to work out the logic to decipher the figures and arrive at the correct answer.

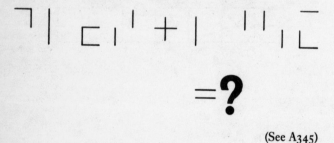

(See A345)

Insert numbers into the remaining blank squares so that all the calculations are correct reading both across and down.

	×		÷		=	12
+		+		+		×
	+		÷	3	=	
÷		÷		−		÷
	+	9	÷		=	
=		=		=		=
4	×		+		=	

(See A354)

Dodecahedra

I have an indefinite number of regular dodecahedra, indistinguishable in appearance from each other. I have pots of red and blue paint. If each face of each dodecahedron* is to be painted red or blue, how many dodecahedra that are distinguishable from one another shall I be able to produce?

* Dodecahedron: a solid figure having twelve plane faces.

(See A374)

Food for Thought

When the following numbers are applied to malt

$$160934.4$$
$$.4046873$$
$$33.81402$$
$$2240.0$$

what is malt converted to?

(See A290)

Start at the top left-hand square and work from square to square horizontally, vertically or diagonally to find the 'Law of the Search'. Visit every square only once and finish at the bottom right-hand square.

T	H	H	E	L	A	A	C
F	E	T	T	S	L	Y	E
L	I	R	S	P	W	U	O
A	P	T	S	I	G	O	U
O	C	E	I	N	P	L	D
L	T	T	H	E	C	X	E
O	K	F	Y	T	T	T	O
O	O	R	A	N	I	B	E

(See A359)

A settler in the island of Helpuselph applied to the Governor for some land.

'How much would you like?' asked the Governor.

'About 100 square miles.'

'OK,' said the Governor. 'You may choose a rectangular parcel of land in the township of Little Rainfall. Its dimensions must be such that if one side of the rectangle were 5 miles longer, and the other 4 miles longer, the area of the rectangle would be twice as great, and its perimeter must be exactly 46 miles.'

The applicant duly selected and fenced his land in accordance with these conditions. But he got away with 6 square miles more than the Governor had anticipated. What was the area of the selected rectangle?

(See A263)

Express 100 as the sum of three cubes, allowing each cube to be positive or negative. There are only three known answers, one of which is:

$$190^3 - 161^3 - 139^3$$

Can you find the other two solutions, one with larger numbers and one with smaller numbers than the solution above?

(See A369)

Insert the 26 letters of the alphabet to complete the crossword. Four of the letters have already been inserted.

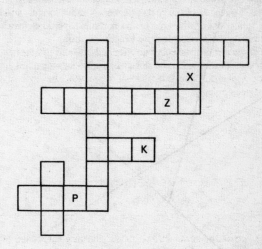

A B C D E F G H I J Ⓚ L M
N O Ⓟ Q R S T U V W Ⓧ Y Ⓩ

(See A360)

289

The largest number of non-overlapping triangles that can be produced by drawing seven straight lines is 11. Your task below is to work out how this can be done. Three lines are already in position, showing just one triangle, and you must add a further four straight lines to the figure to produce the 11 non-overlapping triangles.

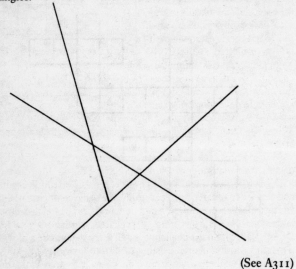

(See A311)

Magic word squares, like magic number squares, have their own special fascination. The famous example on the right is believed to have been engraved on a piece of wall plaster in Roman times and was discovered in 1868 at Cirencester, where it is now exhibited at the Corinium Museum. It is unique because the words read the same not only across and down, as with conventional magic

R	O	T	A	S
O	P	E	R	A
T	E	N	E	T
A	R	E	P	O
S	A	T	O	R

squares, but also backwards and upwards! Never since has anyone, in any language, achieved a magic word square with these properties.

Magic word squares become progressively more difficult to compile as the number of words increases. Several 8 × 8 squares have been achieved and there have been many attempts at nine- and ten-letter squares but, regretfully, these have either contained words for which meanings cannot be found or repeated words and tautonyms (words consisting of repeated words: for example, Baden-Baden). So the challenge is still there to compile a nine- or ten-letter word square consisting of different words with known meanings, a challenge which was, incidentally, issued some three years ago in the British Mensa journal – but no solution was ever received.

The answers to the clues, which are in no particular order, are all five-letter words. When the answers are placed in the correct position in the correct grid, two magic squares will be formed so that the same five words can be read both across and down.

CLUES:

Pendent fleshy part of soft palate

Angry

Authorized

Firm

Former gold coin of Italy

Exhilarate

Valleys

Valued

More vulgar

Work of music

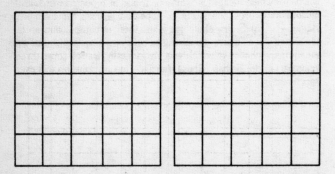

(See A348)

The answers to the clues, which are in no particular order, are all six-letter words. When the answers are placed in the correct position in the correct grid, two magic squares will be formed so that the same six words can be read both across and down.

CLUES:

Drink

Participates

Natural ability

Reach

Buy back

Strike continuously

More emotionally strained

Pared away

Develop gradually

Large piece of landed property

Disinclined

Three-legged stand

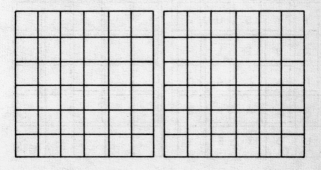

(See A321)

** (a) Insert the 40 letters below into the remaining spaces in the grids to form two 5 × 5 magic squares so that in each grid the same words can be read both across and down.

A, A, A, E, E, E, E, E, E, F, F, H, I, L, L, N, N, O, O, P, P, P, P, R, R, R, R, R, R, S, S, S, S, S, T, T, T, T, W, W

				T
			E	
		I		
	E			
T				

				F
				E
			A	
		E		
F				

(See A287)

* (b) Rearrange the letters to form a magic square where the five words read the same both across and down.

T	Y	S	U	L
K	H	E	L	H
F	A	L	A	O
A	L	A	F	D
L	O	T	E	Y

(See A335)

Next, when you are describing,
A shape, or sound, or tint;
Don't state the matter plainly,
But put it in a hint;
And learn to look at all things,
With a sort of mental squint.
Lewis Carroll

For our final section we have chosen another miscellany of puzzles to test and tease you. We hope you have enjoyed the selection of brainteasers that we have presented you with and that you have been successful in coming up with many of the correct solutions.

When the zoetrope* has been spun into the position below, the word 'ORB' on the outer circle gives the word 'RUE' on the inner circle: this is done by taking the letters O-R-B on the outer circle, then finding their corresponding letters, R-U-E, in the same order on the inner circle.

Using this system with the zoetrope in the same position, find another three-letter word in the outer circle which will also give a three-letter word in the inner circle. Then find a four-letter word. Then find the five-letter name of a reptile on the outer circle which spells out the name of a famous Austrian on the inner circle.

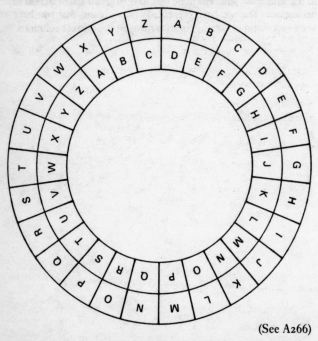

(See A266)

* Zoetrope: A toy with a revolving cylinder which shows a series of pictures as if the subject were alive and moving.

Each couplet provides the clue to a word. Solve the clues and list
the six words. Two more words will be spelt out by the first and last
letters of the six words.

A tiny note, it's in quick time,
All you need to solve this rhyme?

Cry to Mark, it's so abrupt,
Delight or horror will erupt.

Set a course to steer the ship,
Plot the route when off you trip.

Just a drop to come apart,
Joy perhaps, or sad at heart?

Describe a lad who now is striving,
One day his hopes may be arriving.

Sculpture of freedom and all is well,
Here's independence and the marching bell.

(See A297)

Early Arrival

My wife usually leaves work at 4.30 p.m., calls at the supermarket, then catches the 5 p.m. train, which arrives at our home town station at 5.30 p.m. I leave home each day, drive to the station and pick up my wife at 5.30 p.m., just as she gets off the train. One day last week my wife was able to finish work about five minutes earlier than usual, decided to go straight to the station instead of calling at the supermarket and managed to catch the 4.30 p.m. train, which arrived at our home town station at 5 p.m. Because I was not there to pick her up she began to walk home. I left home at the usual time, saw my wife walking, turned round, picked her up and drove home, arriving there 12 minutes earlier than usual. For how long did my wife walk before I picked her up?

(See A373)

*304
Chess Tournament

At an international chess tournament the four semi-finalists, Zena Le Vue, Dr A. Glebe, Rob E. Lumen and Ann Ziata, each represented one of four continents: Europe, Africa, the Americas and Australasia. Can you correctly match each of the four chess masters with the continent which they represented?

(See A336)

What do the answers to the following clues all have in common?

Tract of waste land

Dwelling place

Place of great delight or contentment

A rule

Flake off

Ashen

A cardinal point

(See A267)

Arrange the following into groups of three:

AMITY
  ASTRONOMY
   CONCORD
    COMET
     CHEMISTRY
      DOUGLAS
       HARMONY
        HARRIER
         PEACE
          PLANET
           PHYSICS
           STAR

(See A315)

On a map showing country boundaries, what is the least number of colours required to colour in the map so that adjoining countries have different colours?

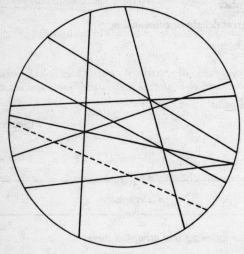

Where countries join at a point they are not considered to be adjoining.

How many colours are required if an additional boundary (shown dotted) is added?

(See A367)

Find 29 names given to groups of animals, birds, fish and objects hidden in the three paragraphs.

In the cove near Hove rafters tend to rake and span and slot home on buildings.

In the same cove your outer charm will be the downfall of a gang of husky gamblers.

You can hear the snide remarks of a wisp of blushing kennel maids as they drift and clamour and mingle and hover and cry at the observance of a dray full of troops.

(See A337)

What letters should replace the question marks below?

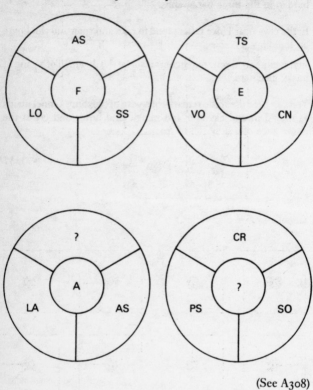

(See A308)

Find the missing square.

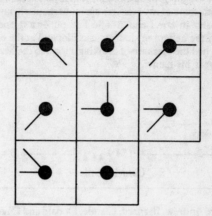

Choose from:

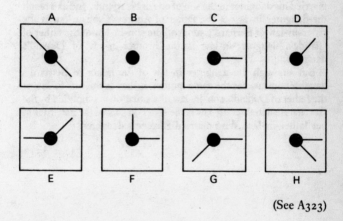

(See A323)

Last week it was the 70th birthday party of my uncle. It was good to meet up with some of my relatives again, particularly my brother, Bert, and sister-in-law, Lena. Auntie Tina put on a splendid buffet supper with the help of my half-cousin Flo, and at the end of the evening we had the pleasure of drinking a toast to the health of my uncle. What is his name?

(See A363)

****312
Coup de Grâce

Five friends, Andrew, Bernard, Claude, Donald and Eugene, each have a son and a daughter. Their families are so close that each has married his daughter to the son of one of his friends, and as a result the daughter-in-law of the father of Andrew's son-in-law is the sister-in-law of Bernard's son, and the son-in-law of the father of Claude's daughter-in-law is the brother-in-law of Donald's daughter.

But although the daughter-in-law of the father of Bernard's daughter-in-law has the same mother-in-law as the son-in-law of the father of Donald's son-in-law, the situation is simplified by the fact that no daughter-in-law is the sister-in-law of the daughter of her father-in-law. Who married Eugene's daughter?

(See A312)

ANSWERS

We hope you managed to arrive at many of the correct answers and that you derived a great deal of satisfaction and pleasure from doing so. We have ensured that all the answers are fully explained, so that for those which you were unable to crack, you will obtain a clear idea of what you should have done to come up with the correct solution. We hope that, in some way, we have added to your store of knowledge and we feel sure that by tackling our compilation you will have increased your puzzle-solving (and hopefully problem-solving) capacities.

A1 (Q70) $1248 - 8 - 4096$
             $428 - 8 - 4096$
             $4812 - 8 - 4096$

The product of the digits of each number in the first column is 64. The second column is the square root of 64. The third column is the square of 64.

A2 (Q32)   (a) $5.5 - 5 \times 55 \times (5 - \frac{5}{5})$ or $\frac{555}{5} - \frac{55}{55}$

         (b) $\dfrac{6^6}{\frac{6}{6} + \frac{6}{6} + 6}$

         (c) $\dfrac{7777 \times 7}{\sqrt{7} \times 7}$

A3 (Q80)   Always four no matter how the grid is drawn.

A4 (Q97)   Screw the threes together to make an eight.

A5 (Q89)   (a) PALPITATE.

         (b) SPINNAKER.

         (c) CLOCKWISE.

         (d) TEMPORARY.

         (e) EXCURSION.

A6 (Q20)   ALBANIA, TIRANA, LEK; AZORES, PONTA DELGADA, ESCUDO; BERMUDA, HAMILTON, DOLLAR; COSTA RICA, SAN JOSE, COLON; GABON, LIBREVILLE, FRANC; GAMBIA, BANJUL, DALASI; GUINEA, CONAKRY, SYLI; HONDURAS, TEGUCIGALPA, LAMPIRA; LAOS, VIENTIANE, KIP; MALDIVE ISLANDS, MALE, RUPEE; MONGOLIA, ULAN BATOR, TUGHRIK; PARAGUAY, ASUNCION, GUARANI; QATAR, DOHA, RIYAL; SUDAN, KHARTOUM, POUND.

A7 (Q26)   (a) CIRCUMNAVIGATION.

              (b) INTERCHANGEABLE.

              (c) TRIGONOMETRICAL.

A8 (Q63)   PRESTIDIGITATION.

A9 (Q39)   (a) Several solutions are possible, but one example is:

695
782
431

or any combination of these numbers in the same columns.

             (b) 40.82
       9.75
       1.63
       52.2

A10 (Q30)   EMPEROR (SOVEREIGN), VISOR (EYESHADE), ORDER (INSTRUCTION), LOVER (SWEETHEART), VILLAGER (INHABITANT), INTELLIGENCER (INFORMANT), NUMBER (AGGREGATE), GEAR (APPARATUS).

A11 (Q4)   Proceed via prime numbers, i.e. 2–3–5–7–11–
            13–17 up to 43.

A12 (Q77)   Both one chance in four.

A13 (Q35)   47637
            22212
            83457
            91782
            45819

A14 (Q34)   To solve this puzzle it is essential to pick up the
            opening clue that there were only *two* prelimi-
            nary rounds, therefore, the number of entries
            for *one* of the competitions must have been
            either 4, 8, 16, 32, 64 etc. so that no preliminary
            rounds were necessary. From there by some
            trial and error it is possible to arrive at the
            following solution, which is the only one which
            meets the requirements of the remainder of the
            puzzle:

Entries	(Cube)	Players in 1st Round	Players in Preliminaries	Preliminary round losers	Matches	My rounds
22	(10648)	10	12	6	21	5
32	(32768)	32	0	0	31	5
42	(74088)	22	20	10	41	6
— 13						
CONSOLATION EVENT						
16		16	0		15	
					— 108 —	— 16 —

My handicap = 8.   My wife's handicap = 16.
Club Statistician's handicap = 13.   Seth
Arkwright's age = 108.

A15 (Q6) (a) HOOD – each word can be prefixed by the word MAN to form another word.

(b) KNOT – all the words have their letters in alphabetical order.

(c) CAUTIONED – all the words contain all five vowels.

A16 (Q13) ANTIGUA, MARTINIQUE, SEYCHELLES, SUDAN, UGANDA, YEMEN, DUBAI, ALGERIA, ANGOLA, INDONESIA, SENEGAL, COLOMBIA, RWANDA. ANAGRAM: DAMASCUS, SYRIA.

A17 (Q82) 32 – number the sides of the first cube 0,1,2,3,5,7. Number the sides of the second cube 0,1,2,4,6,8. The 6 can be turned over and displayed as a 9.

A18 (Q92) (a) V (vowel) 1 = A etc. C (consonant) 1 = B etc. Well done! Message successfully decoded.

(b) A or N = 1, B or O = 2 etc. To all the puzzle solvers who have persevered, patiently (?) to decode this message, congratulations!

A19 (Q22) (a) 3 – product of digits differs.

(b) 4682 – sum digits differs.

A20 (Q45) TRAVELS, LILLIPUT, BROBDINGNAG (GULLIVER)
SWIFT, SWALLOW, MIGRATION (BIRDS).
RAPID, QUICK, FAST (SPEED).
JOURNEY, EXCURSION, EXPEDITION (TRAVEL).

A21 (Q47) TENT.

A22 (Q78) Remember pi to 8 decimal places. The number of letters in each word represents the digits of pi, i.e. 3.14159265.

A23 (Q5) (a) T – i.e. Two-Four-Six etc.

(b) T – i.e. laterally symmetric.

(c) P – i.e. no symmetries.

A24 (Q12) TROJAN WAR, DEATH OF ALEXANDER THE GREAT AT BABYLON, ROMAN INVASION OF BRITAIN, REVOLT OF BOADICEA, DARK AGES, NORMAN CONQUEST OF ENGLAND, MAGNA CARTA SEALED BY KING JOHN, MODEL PARLIAMENT, HUNDRED YEARS WAR, REBELLION OF WAT TYLER, BATTLE OF AGINCOURT, JOAN OF ARC BURNED AT ROUEN, WARS OF ROSES ENDED BY BATTLE OF BOSWORTH, CHRISTOPHER COLUMBUS DISCOVERED AMERICA, SIR FRANCIS DRAKE SAILED ROUND WORLD, GUNPOWDER PLOT, CIVIL WAR IN ENGLAND, OLIVER CROMWELL BECAME LORD PROTECTOR, GREAT FIRE OF LONDON, ACCESSION OF PETER THE GREAT OF RUSSIA, UNION OF ENGLAND AND SCOTLAND, SOUTH SEA BUBBLE.

A25 (Q7) (d) – when two symbols touch, they disappear from the next square and two new symbols are introduced. The remaining two symbols retain their position.

A26 (Q18) CONDUCTOR, CONCERTO, HORNS, CYMBALS, OBOE, BASSOON, STRINGS, CELLO, HARP, PICCOLO, BRASS, PERCUSSION, TROMBONE, ORGAN, FLUTE, TRUMPET, WOODWIND, VIOLA, VIOLIN, TRIANGLE, TUBA, BELLS, DRUMS, BUGLE.

A27 (Q44)   MENDELSSOHN, ELIJAH, HEBRIDES
            (MENDELSSOHN)
            WESTERN ISLES, MINCH,
            STORNOWAY
            (HEBRIDES).
            ISRAEL, JAFFA, ASHDOD (ISRAEL).
            HAYDN, CREATION, SEASONS
            (HAYDN).

A28 (Q68)   15707 – 3.1.44 – 20816
            17079 – 6.10.47 – 19444
            26632 – 1.12.73 – 9891

            The middle column is a date. The first column
            is the number of preceding days this century
            and the last column is the remaining days this
            century. The year 1900 was not a leap year due
            to adjustments on the Gregorian Calendar,
            whereby the leap year is omitted at the turn of
            the century if the year is not divisible by 400,
            therefore, although 1900 was not a leap year,
            the year 2000 will be.

A29 (Q74)   3, 5, 6   – 30 (Least common
                                       multiple)
            9, 15, 20   – 180
            8, 9, 15, 16, 20 – 720

A30 (Q100) NECKLACE.

A31 (Q85)   O, NO, NOT, NOTE, TENOR,
            ORIENT, PROTEIN, INCEPTOR,
            RECEPTION.

A32 (Q19)   (a) 1. MINNESOTA
                2. OKLAHOMA
                3. NEBRASKA
                4. TENNESSEE
                5. ARKANSAS
                6. NEW JERSEY
                7. ALABAMA

'E PLURIBUS UNUM' means 'one out of many' and is the motto of the United States of America.

(b) 0. CALM
     1. LIGHT AIR
     2. SLIGHT BREEZE
     3. GENTLE BREEZE
     4. MODERATE BREEZE
     5. FRESH BREEZE
     6. STRONG BREEZE
     7. MODERATE GALE
     8. FRESH GALE
     9. STRONG GALE
     10. WHOLE GALE
     11. STORM
     12. HURRICANE
ANAGRAM – BEAUFORT SCALE.

A33 (Q23) 4 – the others are part of the International Phonetic Alphabet.

A34 (Q1) Proceed via $3-3^2-3^3-3^4$, i.e. $3-9-27-81-243$ etc.

A35 (Q96) (a) Divides by 11 if the sum of alternate digits is equal.

(b) R/NATIONALISATION.

(c) $(14 + 3)(14 - 3) = 17 \times 11 = 187$.

A36 (Q41) MACMILLAN, PEDAL, BICYCLE (BICYCLE).
LEVER, BAR, ROD (LEVERS).
THATCHER, STRAW, ROOF (THATCHING).
HOME, RESIDENCE, ABODE (WHERE WE LIVE).

A37 (Q49) TENNIS.

A38 (Q73)   (f) – read each line both across and down to
             make a logical sequence. The complete
             solution is:

$$3261—3262—3263$$
$$1623—2623—3623$$
$$4884—5885—6886$$

N.B. $3261 + 1623 = 4884$.

A39 (Q52)   HIGH IQ.

A40 (Q16)   'AMERICAN PRESIDENTS' SPELT OUT
             IN QUESTION: ADAMS, EISENHOWER,
             FORD, FILLMORE, BUCHANAN,
             NIXON, PIERCE, JEFFERSON,
             KENNEDY, HAYES, WILSON,
             CLEVELAND, HOOVER, GRANT,
             TRUMAN, WASHINGTON.

A41 (Q11)   RACHMANINOV, GOUNOD,
             SCHUMANN, BEETHOVEN, ELGAR,
             BIZET, TSCHAIKOVSKY, MASCAGNI,
             SCHUBERT, MENDELSSOHN,
             MEYERBEER, BERLIOZ, PUCCINI,
             STRAVINSKY, WAGNER. ANAGRAM:
             ENIGMA VARIATIONS.

A42 (Q33)   Lines Down:

(A) 1131111		(G) 171776
(B) 443556892		(H) 566784
(C) 735893		(I) 3352273926
(D) 822117882		(J) 552296
(E) 51		(K) 03326672
(F) 221778		(L) 244226

A43   Quotations (i) Introduction anagram – William
             Shakespeare.

A44 (Q55)   BACKWARDSWAY.

A45 (Q79)   9 a.m. – to solve this puzzle you have to realise
             that if the clock strikes at 1-second intervals it
             only takes 10 seconds to strike 11 p.m. because
             it takes only 1 second for the first two strikes.
             Add 11 hours on to 11 p.m. i.e. 10 a.m. but then
             deduct 1 hour due to the clocks being put back
             at the end of British Summer Time and you
             arrive at the time of the appointment, 9 a.m.

A46 (Q71)   (e) – in each vertical column the three words
             use the same four letters. The complete
             solution therefore is:

             EDIT   EMIR   TIME
               | | |
             TIDE   RIME   EMIT
               | | |
             DIET   MIRE   MITE

A47 (Q2)   (b) – to complete every possible pairing of the
             four symbols.

A48 (Q83)   Circle most – triangle least.

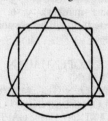

A49 (Q9)   (a) QUARTER – it is the next highest measure
             of capacity.

             (b) DUBLIN – it is part of a State or County
             (represented by *Texas*). Texas is part of a
             Country (represented by *France*). France is part
             of a Continent (represented by *Asia*). Asia is part
             of a Planet (represented by *Neptune*). Neptune
             orbits a Star (represented by *Sirius*).

313

(c) TUBA (ABUT) – all the words form another word when read backwards.

(d) MAD – each word can be prefixed by the word NO to form another word.

A50 (Q27)   (a) ASTROPHYSICS.

(b) ASYMMETRICAL.

(c) TRAPEZIUMS.

A51 (Q24)   NONSENSE (MEANINGLESS), INFINITE (ENDLESS), GAZELLE (ANTELOPE), MANOEUVRE (MOVEMENT), ABORIGINE (AUSTRALIAN), SUBSCRIBE (CONTRIBUTE), IRRITABLE (TROUBLESOME), GRUESOME (FRIGHTFUL).

A52 (Q37)   Starting immediately to the right of the right hand overlapping number and moving clockwise, insert the digits in the grid as follows:

5, 3, 7, 5, 9, 1, 8, 9, 4, 2, 6, 7, 2, 3, 7, 8 (left-hand overlapping number), 3, 1, 5, 6, 4 (8 already inserted), 9, 1, 5, 3, 7 (right-hand overlapping number), 5, 6, 1, 2, 6 (7 already inserted). It will be possible to find other solutions.

A53 (Q46)   NILE, COPENHAGEN, AGAMEMNON (NELSON).
CONGO, NIGER, OBI (RIVERS).
OSLO, HELSINKI, STOCKHOLM (SCANDINAVIAN CAPITALS).
KENYA, KAMET, ELIAS (MOUNTAINS).

A54 (Q81)   He would pay slightly less. 1 inch square = *1 cu. in.* volume or 6 sq. in. area. 1.26 inch square cube = *2 cu. in.* volume or 9.5256 sq. in. area. To double the volume would require approximately 58.75 per cent increase in cardboard, i.e. the percentage increase from 6 to 9.5256. For every £100 worth of cardboard he would now have to pay £158.75, but the discount of 37.5 per cent on the new figure reduces the cost to £99.22.

A55 (Q72) (g) – (o = 1, T = 2) Magic 9 (each line, vertical, horizontal or diagonal, adds up to 9).

A56 (Q10) (a) – the secret of this puzzle is that there are three different elements in each circle which move in a different but logical sequence on a white background, numbered 1–8. The striped element simply moves one position anti-clockwise, then back again clockwise. The black element moves one position clockwise, then two clockwise, then three clockwise, and continues increasing its number of movements by one each time. The most complex movement is of the dotted element. This first moves one position anti-clockwise, then two positions anti-clockwise, but then changes direction and moves back one position clockwise, then two positions clockwise, then changes direction again and continues in this manner.

A57 (Q17) BATTLE OF PRESTON PANS, BLACK HOLE OF CALCUTTA, CAPTURE OF QUEBEC BY WOLFE, SPINNING JENNY INVENTED BY JAMES HARGREAVES, AMERICAN WAR OF INDEPENDENCE, GEORGE WASHINGTON BECOMES FIRST PRESIDENT OF UNITED STATES, OUTBREAK OF FRENCH REVOLUTION, BATTLE OF NILE, NAPOLEON BONAPARTE BECOMES EMPEROR OF FRANCE, INVASION OF RUSSIA BY NAPOLEON, BATTLE OF WATERLOO, THE CRIMEAN WAR, THE AMERICAN CIVIL WAR, PROCLAMATION OF QUEEN VICTORIA

AS EMPRESS OF INDIA, TELEPHONE
INVENTED BY ALEXANDER GRAHAM
BELL, REVISED VERSION OF NEW
TESTAMENT PUBLISHED, BEGINNING
OF THE BOER WAR.

A58 (Q42)   CORSICA, ELBA, ST. HELENA
(NAPOLEON).
SARDINIA, CRETE, CYPRUS (MED.
ISLANDS).
ARGON, GALLIUM, XENON
(ELEMENTS).
ZEBU, ELAND, CHAMOIS (MAMMALS).

A59 (Q38)   (a) YES, by screwing 6 on upside down.

(b) Not without a saw.

A60 (Q69)   (f) each square contains three circles of differ-
ing sizes.

A61 (Q75)   (b) (There are four concentric circles with their
centre at the centre point of the middle
square.)

A62 (Q50)   BLINK.

A63 (Q95)   (a) V for violet (colours of the rainbow).

(b) C for Catherine Parr (Henry VIII's wives).

A64 (Q3)   (a) 256 – it is the square of the sum of the digits
of the preceding number, i.e. $(1 + 6 + 9)^2$.

(b) 26496 – a complex but logical sequence
which progresses as follows: 126 $(12 \times 6) = 72$
$\times (1 + 2 + 6) = 648$ $(64 \times 8) = 512 \times (6 + 4$
$+ 8) = 9216$ $(92 \times 16) = 1472 \times (9 + 2 + 1 +$
$6) = 26496$.

(c) 96 – rearrange the digits 864 in every possible way, then divide each resulting number by
9.

A65 (Q8)   (c) – to solve this puzzle it is first necessary to realise that the arms attached to the central vertical line move round clockwise in the next drawing. This rules out option (b). Secondly, as the top circle and bottom square never change, option (f) can be discounted. The third, and most complex, part of the puzzle is working out the sequence of the symbols to the left and right of the main horizontal line. In the second drawing the left and right symbols from the first drawing have merged at the left-hand side and a new symbol has been introduced on the right. In the third drawing the symbols which merged have now moved out of the drawing, the cross has moved over to the left and a new figure, a circle, has been introduced. The sequence is then repeated, i.e. in the fourth drawing the cross and circle have merged on the left and the new symbol (—) is introduced. The answer, therefore, is (c) where the cross/circle combination has disappeared, symbol (—) has moved over to the left and a completely new symbol (.) has been introduced.

A66 (Q21)   (a) TRAIN (others are anagrams of countries).

(b) LEASED (others pair, i.e. DIRECT/CREDIT using the same letters).

A67 (Q31)   (a) 6842
3762
4367
7447

(b) 2981
3124
4136
3993

A68 (Q43) You should have grouped them in threes each totalling 1000.

A69 (Q36) (a) 16, 24 – they are the factors of the final number 96.

(b) 91 – start at 0 and add progressive square numbers, i.e.
$$0 + 1 = 1, \quad 1 + 4 = 5, \quad 5 + 9 = 14,$$
$$14 + 16 = 30, \quad 30 + 25 = 55,$$
$$55 + 36 = 91, \quad 91 + 49 = 140.$$

(c) 18 – they are the factors of the final number 36.

A70 (Q15) JAY, MAGPIE, CORMORANT, CUCKOO, ROBIN, ORIOLE, MALLARD, LINNET, LAPWING, WREN, PARTRIDGE, REDWING, LARK, SPARROW, DOVE, REEVE, SWAN, PARROT, ROOK, ROC, LANNER, TERCEL, KA, SORA, GANNET, GOWK, LOON, RAIL, REEDLING, RINGTAIL, SERIN, COB.

A71 (Q53) DESPAIR.

A72 (Q66) When you successfully complete this puzzle you will have proved beyond doubt qualities of determination and patience.

A73 (Q76) 232 entries – 229 matches were played, therefore there must have been 229 losers. Add the two who scratched out without playing and then add the winner of the Championship and you arrive at the total number of entries – 232.

A74 (Q94) (a) 6 – look at a typewriter.

(b) 7 – to spell Morse Code.

A75 (Q88) A, AT, ATE, LATE, LATER, RELATE, RELATED, RETAILED, LIBERATED, DELIBERATE.

A76 (Q90)   JOBS, OF, NYMPHS, ZYGAL,
            QUART, TWICE, KID, VEX.

A77 (Q25)   NARCISSI, NERINE (BULBOUS),
            IMMEDIATE, IMPENDING (IMMINENT),
            GALVANISM, GENERATE
            (ELECTRICAL), MANTLE, MANTILLA
            (GARMENT), ATROCIOUS, ABOMINATE
            (UNPLEASANT), SCAMPI, SARDINE
            (AQUATIC), IMPOLITE, INSULTING
            (DISCOURTEOUS), GORGE, GRABEN
            (GEOLOGICAL).

A78 (Q40)   *Across*   *Down*

            A. 13824   A. 10648
            E. 16   B. 85184
            G. 405224   C. 44100
            H. 68121   D. 357911
            I. 9801   E. 125000
            L. 81   F. 64
            M. 592704   J. 59319
            P. 64000   K. 17576
            Q. 2197   L. 8464
            R. 5625   N. 7056
                              O. 3025

A79 (Q93)   The key is as follows:

A B C D E F G H I J K L M N O P Q R S T U V W X Y Z
| | | | | | | | | | | | | | | | | | | | | | | | | |
M K Z H I O Q R A V T G Y W U F B C L X J D E S N P

Decoded, the message reads:

Trying to identify double letter words and
common endings such as 'ER' and 'ING' can be
of considerable assistance when attempting to
decode messages of this type. Additional information, for example, knowing that the letter 'E'
is the most common letter in the English language and that 'ING' is the most common three
letter word ending is also worth knowing.

A80 (Q14)   FINE DRIZZLE, DRY SHERRY, AWFULLY GOOD, SLIPPED UP, SWEET SORROW, GOOD GRIEF, STAND DOWN, STANDING JUMP, RETIRED PERMANENT SECRETARY, FUTURE HISTORY, SIT UP, WAR GAMES, SPEND THRIFT, PERFECTLY AWFUL, ADVANCE TO THE REAR, ADVANCED BEGINNERS, FEELING NUMB, BITTER SWEET, LOOSE FIT, HOT CHILLI, BAD GOODS.

A81 (Q28)   AGGRAVATING (EXASPERATING), LINING (COVERING), LONG (EXTENSIVE), OBLONG (RECTANGULAR), PANG (COMPUNCTION), ENTERING (REGISTERING), ROLLICKING (BOISTEROUS), SCRYING (FORETELLING).

A82 (Q67)

$$7 \times 4 \times 8 \times 6 \times 2 - 2 \times 6 \times 8 \times 8 - 768$$

82687	-5376	-630
79988	-36288	-2304

A83 (Q91)

(a) Queen Elizabeth, Spanish Armada defeated, back soon with treasure. Francis Drake.

(b) Mark Antony, milkman delivered, please drop by tonight and scrub my back. Cleopatra.

A84 (Q57)

(a) All things come to him who will but wait – Longfellow.
Forget forgive conclude and be agreed – Shakespeare.

(b) Absence makes the heart grow fonder – Bayly.
The only way to have a friend is to be one – Emerson.

A85 (Q60) The only people who do not make mistakes are those who do nothing and that is the greatest mistake of all.

A86 (Q98) (e) – the initial letters spell out P I C K S A I L.

A87 (Q56) UPSIDE DOWN.

A88 (Q48) ENCIRCLE.

A89 (Q86) SKY, JUMPY, QUARTZ, THONG, FOX, GLIB, VICE, DEW.

A90 (Q29) (a) PANTOGRAPHIC.

  (b) METAMORPHOSIS.

  (c) ARCHAEOLOGICAL.

A91 (Q58) There is in the worst of fortune the best chances for a happy change – Euripides.

A92 (Q99) GAS/SLAVE/LAS VEGAS. 'Las Vegas' uses the same eight letters which appear in the words 'Gas' and 'Slave'.

A93 (Q87) (a) ALTER – ALERT – LATER
  (b) SEPAL – LEAPS – PLEAS
  (c) REMIT – MITRE – TIMER
  (d) SLIME – SMILE – MILES
  (e) KILNS – SLINK – LINKS
  (f) RESET – STEER – TREES

A94 (Q84) (a) MISUNDERSTANDING.

  (b) CIRCUMFERENCE.

A95 (Q62) The square numbers are:

  Across – 1296, 5184, 8649, 6241, 8464, 529, 2025, 1225, 49, 169, 36.
  Down – 25, 16, 8281, 144, 1521, 256, 6889, 64, 4624, 9409, 576.

A96 (Q54)   WIRING.

A97 (Q61)   Your rewards for this effort are satisfaction and congratulations. Anagram: Nothing.

A98 (Q51)   COLONEL.

A99 (Q64)   Words are: MOP, END, COVET, SKYLIGHT, FRY, JIB, SQUAW, ZAX.

A100 (Q59) (a) The end of labour is to gain leisure – Aristotle.

(b) A spark neglected makes a mighty fire – Herrick.

A101 (Q65)
7	13	4	10
2	12	5	15
9	3	14	8
16	6	11	1

A102 (Q117) Across: 2. Man, 4. Begot, 6. Paraded, 8. Hare, 9. Elan, 11. Role, 12. Lies, 14. Beta, 15. Reed, 16. Deck, 18. Side, 19. Leaf, 21. Apes, 22. Sleeves, 24. Elbow, 25. Low.
Down: 1. Saga, 2. Mere, 3. Node, 4. Bare, 5. Tell, 6. Palaces, 7. Dairies, 8. Hotel, 10. Needs, 11. Red, 13. See, 17. Kale, 18. Spew, 20. Fell, 21. Avow, 23. Ebon.

A103 (Q102c) $428 + 533 = 961, 566 + 127 = 693, 361 + 414 = 775, 565 + 196 = 761$.

A104   (Cryptograms, Introduction)
'What hat's that?' said Bill.
'The flat hat,' said Ben.
'Oh, that hat,' said Bill.
'That's that then.'

A105 (Q111)   You win £59. You will always win the same number of units that heads comes down in the sequence, providing the final toss is heads.

A106 (Q150a)   Fragmentary.

A107 (Q153)   52938
49617
78453
97722
21177

A108   (Brainbenders for Mentalathletes, Introduction) 2^{60}.

A109 (Q145)   (a) Couples Flirting (b) Muttering through Moustache.

A110 (Q113)   In a pack of 52 cards there are 32 cards of nine or below. The chance that the first card dealt is one of the 32 is $\frac{32}{52}$, the second card $\frac{31}{51}$ etc.
The chance of all 13 being favourable is $\frac{32}{52} \times \frac{31}{51} \ldots \frac{20}{40}$ or $\frac{1}{1828}$.
The odds were strongly in Lord Yarborough's favour.

A111 (Q128)   It is pi to nine decimal places: 3.141592654.

A112 (Q141)   121 – 111211 – 311221. Each number describes the previous number, i.e. 121 then 1-1, 1-2, 1-1, then 3-1s, 1-2, 2-1s.

A113 (Q132)   At some time during the calculation you will be multiplying by (x-x), which equals 0, therefore the product will be 0.

A114 (Q115)   2/1. The number of pictures on the card does not affect the odds.

A115 (Q134)   When the metal was taken out of the bowl, the bowl displaced less water, so the water level fell by an amount corresponding to the volume of water which would have the same weight as the metal. When the metal was immersed in the water, it displaced its own volume of water and the water level rose. The amount it rose corresponded to the volume of the metal, very much less than the volume of an equal weight of water. Hence the net result was a fall in water level.

A116 (Words (ii) introduction)
    (a) Bookkeeper.
    (b) Raised/Razed.
    (c) Uncopyrightable or Dermatoglyphics.
    (d) Euphoria, Equation
    (e) Underground, Entertainment.
    (f) Onomatopoeia.
    (g) Sovereignty.
    (h) Desserts/Stressed.
    (i) Facetious, Abstemious, Uncomplimentary, Subcontinental.

A117 (Q103b) Tutor: its letters are contained in instructor in the correct order as with destruction/ruin.

A118 (Q101c) (i) IOE. They are the vowels extracted from the colours of the rainbow – red, orange, yellow, green, blue, indigo, violet.
(ii) AUA. They are the vowels extracted from the days of the week – Sunday, Monday, Tuesday, Wednesday, Thursday, Friday, Saturday.

A119 (Q156) 2: The initial letters of the others spell out musical instruments – flute, harp, tuba.

A120 (Q139) He puts down 4 × 10p and 2 × 5p coins. If he had required Jubilee he would have put down 4 × 10p and 1 × 5p coins.

A121 (Q103c) Maid. All words can be prefixed with BAR to form another word.

A122 (Q163) Crypt, Rhythm, Tryst, Hymn, Nymph.

A123 (Anagrams Galore, Introduction) Somersault.

A124 (Q173)

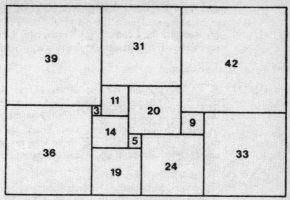

A125 (Q185)   Thou art a summer bird which ever in the haunch of
winter sings. The lifting up of day.
A rarer spirit never Did steer humanity;
but you, Gods,
will give us Some faults to make us men.

A126 (Q121)   **Across: Disused, Tornado, Unequal, Sunless.**
Down: Detours, Surgeon, Stature, Doodles.

A127 (Q180)   3.67
         18.745
          1.096
        14.8
        ——————
        38.311

A128 (Q162c)   Circulate.

A129 (Q177) $98 - 76 + 54 + 3 + 21 = 100$.

A130 (Q183a)   All knowledge is but remembrance – (Plato).
All learning is but recollection – (Socrates).

A131 (Q101d)   **Above** the line. Straight letters go above; curved
letters below.

A132 (Q105) (d) So that each corner sub-square of each of the four main sections has a line missing.

A133 (Q149) (a) Racoon, (b) Leopard, (c) Terrier, (d) Lioness, (e) Samoyed, (f) Spaniel, (g) Carthorse, (h) Africa lion.

A134 (Q138) When parking his car the driver of car F had unknowingly stopped touching the front bumper of a car parked in space E. Being in a hurry for the game, he forgot to pull on the handbrake. When, later, the driver of car E backed out there was no longer anything to hold car F and it rolled forward into car C.

A135 (Q124) How often have I said to you that when you have eliminated the impossible, whatever remains, *however improbable,* must be the truth?

(Conan) Doyle

Message keyed: (ELMNTARYDWSO) – Elementary, my dear Watson.

A136 (Q131) 17 (seventeen): All numbers containing only 'E' vowels.

A137 (Q147) Incommensurable.

A138 (Q110) Looking across, the curved lines merge and the straight lines disappear. Looking down, the reverse happens. The missing square is, therefore, (f).

A139 (Q155a) They contain their square root, i.e. 3600, 5776; 2500 is the other four-figure number sharing this feature.

A140 (Q151b) Ptarmigan (Tramp Gain), Starling (Grin Last), Wagtail (Wait Lag), Fieldfare (Feed Frail), Shoveler (Love Hers), Partridge (Grip Trade), Pheasant (Heat Pans).

A141 (Q120) 1. Pictorial, 2. Lorgnette, 3. Explosive, 4. Engender, 5. Reniform, 6. Modicum, 7. Muffled, 8. Drool, 9. Lolling, 10. Geysers, 11. Selling, 12. Gald, 13. Dosed, 14. Dew, 15. Were, 16. Elan, 17. Nod.

A142 (Q158) (c) All the others are symmetric about a horizontal axis, i.e. they appear the same turned upside down.

A143 (Q101e) F.A.A.N. They are the initials of the months of the year.

A144 (Q116) 720, i.e. 6! or $6 \times 5 \times 4 \times 3 \times 2 \times 1$.

A145 (Q102a) (i) 529; 841. They are the squares of progressive prime numbers.
(ii) 10. i.e. $9 \times 7 \times 3 \times 7 \times 6 = 7938$. $7 \times 9 \times 3 \times 8 = 1512$. $1 \times 5 \times 1 \times 2 = 10$.
(iii) 3125. i.e. 5^5. The sequence is 1^1, 2^2, 3^3, 4^4, 5^5.
(iv) 2574. It is the odd numbers from the previous number multiplied by the even numbers, i.e. 99×26.
(v) 792. It is the square numbers from the previous number multiplied by the remaining numbers, i.e. 9×88.

A146 (Odd One Out (ii) introduction)

Abort	(it is five letters long.)
Act	(Last letter cannot be placed first to form another word.)
Agt	(Not an actual word.)
Alp	(Does not end in 'T'.)
Opt	(Does not start with 'A')
Apt	(Not in alphabetical order with rest.)

A147 (Q190c) 105.

A148 (Q198) SX: Each square contains the first and last letters of the numbers one to nine positioned in such a way so as to form a magic square where each horizontal, vertical and corner-to-corner line totals 15.

A149 (Q199) Lines across: India, Peru, Turkey, Kenya, Malta, Nigeria, Italy, Japan, Spain, Cyprus.
Lines down: Mali, Panama, Fiji, Niger, Iran, Cuba, Burma, Canada, Haiti, Togo.

A150 (Q179) 976. Take 2 to the power which gives the lowest number above 1000, which is $2^{10} = 1024$.
Formula = $1024 - \{(1024-1000) \times 2\} = 976$.

A151 (Q192)   Three hours. After x hours,
              A had burned $\frac{x}{6}$ leaving $\frac{6-x}{6}$
              B had burned $\frac{x}{4}$ leaving $\frac{4-x}{4}$
              But after x hours, A was twice as long as B.
              Therefore $\frac{6-x}{6} = \frac{2(4-x)}{4}$ Therefore x = 3.

A152 (Q162d) Reservoir.

A153 (Q181b)

A154 (Q137)   1, 4, 9, 6, 1, 5, 10, 4, 2., Now change to Roman
              numerals: I, IV, IX, VI, I, V, X, IV, II.

A155 (Q107)   (b) The outer dot moves clockwise, first by one
              position, then two positions, then three, etc. The
              inner dot moves anti-clockwise, first by one position,
              then two positions, then three, etc.

A156 (Q160)   (e) It is the only one where the dot is inside the circle.

A157 (Q151a) Policeman (Ample Coin), Mechanic (Came Chin),
              Teacher (The Care), Carpenter (Rap Centre),
              Doctor (To Cord), Secretary (Try Crease),
              Shoemaker (Shake More).

A158 (Q104b) Certainty. The sum of the digits 1-8 is 36. Any
              number divides by 9 exactly when the sum of its
              digits also divides by 9 exactly. It does not matter in
              which order the balls are drawn out as the sum will
              always be 36.

A159 (Q184a) Too much rest is rust – (Walter) Scott.

A160 (Q123)   1. Paled, 2. Azure, 3. Lucre, 4. Erred, 5. Deeds, 6.
              Trade, 7. Riled, 8. Alibi, 9. Debit, 10. Edits, 11.
              State, 12. Tutor, 13. Atone, 14. Tonic, 15. Erect, 16.
              Masse, 17. Aches, 18. Shops, 19. Sepia, 20. Essay,
              21. Tramp, 22. Racer, 23. Acute, 24. Metes, 25.
              Press.

A161 (Q143) (a) Segregate, (b) Charisma, (c) Meteor, (d) Policeman, (e) Silhouette, (f) Doorbell, (g) Married, (h) Matrimony, (i) Sweetheart, (j) Fluster.

A162 (Q103a) They each contain three adjacent consecutive letters of the alphabet, e.g. *stu*dio.

A163 (Q150c) Tergiversation.

A164 (Q114) There are six possible pairings of the four balls: red/red, red(1)/yellow, red(2)/yellow, red(1)/blue, red(2)/blue and yellow/blue. We know the yellow/blue combination has not been drawn out. This leaves five possible combinations remaining, therefore the chances that the red/red pairing has been drawn out are 1 in 5.

A165 (Q184c) All bad precedents began as justifiable measures – Julius Caesar.

A166 (Q176) $\dfrac{5832}{17496}$

A167 (Q101b) T. They are initials of odd numbers; one, three, five, etc.

A168 (Q155b) Their two halves added together equal their square root, i.e. 2025 (20 + 25 = 45) and 45^2 = 2025. The other four-figure number sharing this feature is 3025.

A169 (Q165)

Solution 1		Solution 2	
Vehicle	– Tank	Vehicle	– Tractor
Turret	– Castle	Turret	– Tank
Sand	– Bank	Sand	– Castle
Riparian	– River	Riparian	– Bank
Severn	– Bridge	Severn	– River
Yarborough	– Cards	Yarborough	– Bridge
Jack	– Wood	Jack	– Cards
Yew	– Bow	Yew	– Wood
Arrow	– Bull's-eye	Arrow	– Bow
Farm	– Tractor	Farm	– Bull's-eye

A170 (Q187)   Spad. The remainder are the first three letters of a country followed by the first letter of its capital. Chile-Santiago, Denmark-Copenhagen, France-Paris, Peru-Lima, Portugal-Lisbon.

A171 (Q168)   Across: 1. Jug, 2. Cuscus, 3. Succumb, 4. Zulu, 5. Succubus, 6. Cumulus, 7. Putt.
Down: 1. Truss, 2. Gurus, 3. Cusp, 4. Stuff, 5. Pump, 6. Ruff, 7. Chuck.

A172 (Q174)   Add the percentages together, which gives $80 + 85 + 74 + 68 = 307$ among 100 pupils. This gives 3 losses each and 4 losses to 7 pupils. The least percentage is, therefore, 7.

A173 (Q170)   1. Bethel, 2. Animus, 3. Cayman, 4. Escrow, 5. Hubris, 6. Kibitz, 7. Modish, 8. Pumice, 9. Rimose, 10. Sachet, 11. Turgid, 12. Vagary, 13. Wampum, 14. Torpor, 15. Zephyr, 16. Torque.

A174 (Q164)   1. Wave, 2. Limerick, 3. Zone, 4. Dough, 5. Joy, 6. Pyre, 7. Zebra, 8. Qualify, 9. Exist.

A175 (Q171)   Half of 'What I'd be' must be a whole number. 'What I'd be' must be an even number. 'What I am' cannot end in 1. There are four possible arrangements of the three digits.

	(a)	(b)	(c)	(d)
'What I am'	1?3	13?	31?	?13
'What I'd be'	3?4	34?	43?	?34

'What I am' is 'Nine less than half what I'd be'.
So ('What I am' + 9) × 2 = 'What I'd be'.
Examination shows that only 'A' fits the bill and 'What I am' must be 183.

A176 (Q161)   (c) It is the only cross that will not fit snugly inside a
1 in square.

a 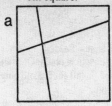   b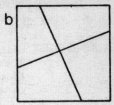

c 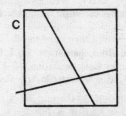   d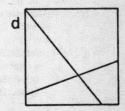

A177 (Q183b)   To err is human, to forgive, divine.   (Pope).
You have two ears; hear both sides of the question.
(Spurgeon)

A178 (Q167)   Grammar. Each word starts with the letter whose
position in the alphabet coincides with the number of
letters in the preceding word, i.e. 'THAT' has four
letters; therefore the next word starts with the fourth
letter in the alphabet – D.

A179 (Q146b)

    (i)   Charles Dickens   (ii) Hans Christian Anderson
    (iii Charlotte Bronte   (iv) Tennessee Williams
    (v)   Charles Lamb   (vi) Robert Louis Stevenson
    (vii) Somerset Maugham

A180 (Q162b)   Enumerate.

A181 (Q104a)   One in 1024. Each spin is an even chance; i.e. 1 in 2.
To repeat 10 times is 1 in 2^{10}.

A182 (Q118) Nestles   Lantern
             Entrant   Engorge
             Strange   Sterner
             Traitor

A183 (Q184b) Old friends are best – Selden.
             The complete quotation reads: Old friends are best.
             King James used to call for his old shoes; they were
             easiest for his feet.

                                        John Selden (1584-1654)

A184 (Q129) $-40°C = -40°F$.

A185 (Q194) Roy, Tuesday, Terry, Wednesday. The names
             appear in alphabetical order, as do the days of the
             week.

A186 (Q148) (a) Militarism, (b) Legalisation, (c) Infection, (d)
             Protectionism, (e) Commendation, (f) Revelations,
             (g) Anarchists, (h) Adversaries, (i) Enormity, (j)
             Desecration.

A187 (Q127) Nothing is as easy as it looks. Everything takes
             longer than you expect. If anything can go wrong, it
             will do so; and always at the worst possible moment.
                                        Murphy's Law
             Message keyed: (PRESONGADL) – Press on
             regardless.

A188 (Q175) Pam has twins aged 3 and triplets aged 1, i.e.
             $3×3×1×1×1 = 3+3+1+1+1$. Fran has triplets
             aged 2 and twins aged 1, i.e. $2×2×2×1×1 =
             2+2+2+1+1$.

A189 (Q108) (d) To complete every possible grouping in threes of
             the four different symbols.

A190 (Q146a) (i) George Washington, (ii) Abraham Lincoln, (iii)
             Herbert Hoover, (iv) Woodrow Wilson, (v) Calvin
             Coolidge, (vi) Theodore Roosevelt, (vii) Franklin
             Delano Roosevelt.

A191 (Q152) 123   789
             456 or 456 or rotations of same
             789   123

A192 (Q130)   9 below, 10 above. Numbers appearing above the line are spelt with three letters only.

A193 (Q126)   Awaiting the sensation of a short sharp shock.
From a cheap and chippy chopper on a big black block.

W. S. Gilbert
(The Mikado)

Word keyed (ALITERON) Alliteration.

A194 (Q104d)   Jim wins £26 + £39 + £47 = £112.
Sid wins £12 + £23 + £21 = £56.
Alf wins £15 + £52 + £65 = £132.

A195 (Q125)   It is known to many that we need solitude to find ourselves. Perhaps it is not so well known that we need solitude to find our fellows. Even the Saviour is described as reaching mankind through the wilderness.

Havelock Ellis

Message keyed (HIDEANSK) Hide and Seek.

A196 (Q190b)   59.

A197   (Brainbenders for Mentalathletes introduction). 840.

A198 (Q191)   73. It is spelt with 12 letters. The previous number is spelt with 11 letters etc.

A199 (Q162e)   Intricate.

A200 (Q136)   The grid should contain 1×1, 2×2, 3×3, 4×4, 5×5, 6×6, 7×7 and 8×8. The missing numbers are, therefore, 5, 6, 8, 8 and all numbers are placed in the grid so that the same number is never horizontally or vertically adjacent.

A201 (Q109)   (a) 3. The only one in which the dot could go in both circle and triangle.
(b) 5. The only one in which the dot could go in all three circles.
(c) 2. The only one that is an asymmetrical figure.

333

        (d) 4. The only one in which the two halves of the
            square are a mirror image, assuming the dividing
            line is a mirror.

        (e) 5. The only one in which one dot could go in one
            square only and one dot in two square only.

A202 (Q112)   Nil. If three are correct then four must be.

A203 (Q154b)   9218
                 7436
                 3531
                 5313

A204 (Q122)   Grid One: Across – Jumpy, Thong, Vice.
               Down – Quartz, Sky, Fox, Glib, Dew.
               Grid Two: Across – Junky, Twigs, Come.
               Down – Quartz, Ply, Fib, Shod, Vex.

A205 (Q142)   (E) The preceding letters are the vowels extracted
               from the question!

A206 (Q196)   M ini M
               E ffend I
               N otio N
               S oun D
               A xi S

A207 (Q172)   Children $2-5-8-11-14-17-20-23-26$
               i.e. $2^2(4) + 5^2(25) + 8^2(64) + 11^2(121) + 14^2(196)$
               $+ 17^2(289) + 20^2(400) + 23^2(529) + 26^2(676)$
               $= 48^2(2304)$.

A208 (Q190a)   23.

A209 (Q101a)   (i) P. The initial of the planets in order from the
sun. Mercury, Venus, Earth, Mars, Jupiter, Saturn, Uranus,
Neptune, Pluto.
(ii) X. A list of letters in the alphabet which are also Roman
numerals.
(iii) S. The initials of the seven deadly sins: Pride, Wrath, Envy,
Lust, Gluttony, Avarice, Sloth.

A210 (Q178) $9 + 8 + 7 + 6 \div 5 - 4 - 3 + 2 - 1 = 0$.

A211 (Q162a)   Telephone.

A212 (Q104c)   Liam (i.e. Mail reversed). Dennis Sinned, Delia Ailed and Tessa had an asset.

A213 (Q154a)   5313
6138
4389
3564

A214 (Q102b)   857, 859. Re-arrange the digits of 7731 in every possible way and then divide the resultant number by 9.

A215 (Q106)   (e) There are two black arms – one moves through 90° each time and the other through 45°. The dotted line never moves but is covered by the black arms when they coincide with its position.

A216 (Q157a)   Aim. All the others contain silent letters.

A217 (Q140)   He had already sugared the tea. When the waiter returned with the supposedly fresh cup, he sugared it again and knew it was the original tea as soon as he took the first sip.

A218 (Q133)   Answer 604. Turn your calculator upside down and it spells hog!

A219 (Q150b)   Transpontine.

A220 (Q103d)   (i) Maritime, (ii) Forsaken, (iii) Convened.

A221 (Q169)   (a) Hell, (b) Soon, (c) Fresh, (d) Effete, (e) Push, (f) Sever, (g) Alone, (h) Adored, (i) Recite, (j) Elegant, (k) Recreant, (l) Doyen, (m) Loiter, (n) New.

A222 (Q182)   For these fellows of infinite tongue, that can rhyme themselves into ladies' favours, they do always reason themselves out again.
King Henry V, vii.162

A223 (Q157b) Sing. All the other words have two pronunciations.

A224 (Q166) They all begin with 'TEN': Tenet, Tentacle, Tenacious, Tench, Tender, Tennis, Tenter, Tenuous, Tenor, Tenantable.

A225 (Q197) Freighter, Yacht, Tanker, Sloop, Trawler, Frigate, Junk, Ketch.

A226 (Q190d) 111.

A227 (Q102d) 72. The number at the top is one quarter of the sum of the two numbers below.

A228 (Q200) (a) Whimsy, (b) Slapstick, (c) Banter, (d) Caricature, (e) Buffoonery, (f) Burlesque, (g) Jocularity, (h) Spoof, (i) Badinage, (j) Satire, (k) Farce, (l) Cartoon, (m) Hoax, (n) Comedy.

A229 (Q188) To fall and not touch a line the card must fall so that the centre of the card falls within the shaded area.

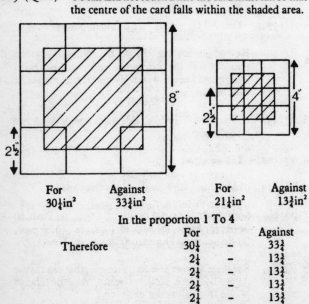

For	Against	For	Against
$30\frac{1}{4}$in^2	$33\frac{3}{4}$in^2	$21\frac{1}{4}$in^2	$13\frac{3}{4}$in^2

In the proportion 1 To 4

	For		Against
Therefore	$30\frac{1}{4}$	–	$33\frac{3}{4}$
	$2\frac{1}{4}$	–	$13\frac{3}{4}$
	$2\frac{1}{4}$	–	$13\frac{3}{4}$
	$2\frac{1}{4}$	–	$13\frac{3}{4}$
	$2\frac{1}{4}$	–	$13\frac{3}{4}$
	$39\frac{1}{4}$		$88\frac{3}{4}$

157   to   355
For   Against

A230 (Q195)   Rain is an anagram of Iran; plane is an anagram of Nepal; chain is an anagram of China.

A231 (Q181a)   Several solutions are possible, for example

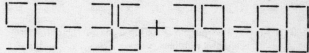

A232 (Q189)   Jemimas, Lupus, Macabre, Nacre, Pilaster, Posse, Punnet, Quoin, Azalea, Sept, Velveteen, Toxophilite, Xenon, Yashmak, Ouija, Sepia.

A233 (Q144)   Cautioned
Auctioned
Education

A234   (Wind-ups, introduction)   MENSA
MENSE
MEUSE
MOUSE
MOULE
MOULD
WOULD
WORLD

A235 (Q193)   220 and 284; i.e. 220 + 110 + 55 + 44 + 22 + 20 + 11 + 10 + 5 + 4 + 2 + 1 = 504
284 + 142 + 71 + 4 + 2 + 1 = 504

A236 (Q186)   Arquebus/Field/Flintlock (All guns)
Atoll/Islet/Key (All islands)
Board/Note/Stone (All can be prefixed with KEY)
Canal/Door/Gun (All have locks)

A237 (Q135)   They should tip the barrel onto its edge until the rum reaches the rim. If they can then see part of the bottom of the barrel, the barrel is not half full. If they cannot see part of the bottom of the barrel, it is more than half full.

A238 (Q119)   1.E. Sauces, 1.S.E. Sonata, 1.N.E. Severe, 2.S. Errata, 2.S.E. Erases, 3.N.E. Agents, 4.E. Era, 4.S. Etna, 4.S.W. Eves, 4.N.E. Ere, 5.W. Are, 5.S. Ache, 6.N. Ante, 6.E. Ate, 7.E. Vets, 7.S. Van, 8.E. Noon, 9.S. Sen, 10.N.E. Gents, 11.S.E. Rases.

A239 (Q159)   All the dots except the one on the extreme right are in orbiting groups around a central dot.

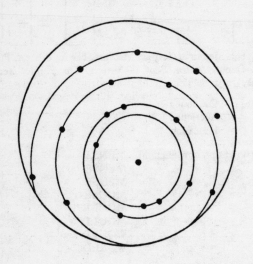

A240 (Q224) 14.7 times (the sum of $1 + 6/5 + 6/4 + 6/3 + 6/2 + 6/1$)

A241 (Q208) Tabulate the results to equal 71. Only three ways are mathematically possible:
25–20–20–3–2–1
25–20–10–10–5–1
50–10–5–3–2–1
The first row is Victor's.
The third row is Madsen's; he hit the bull's-eye.

A242 (Q231) More than 50 per cent.

A243 (Q220b) 2394/16758

A244 (Q253) 'The last thing one discovers in writing a book is what to put first.' Blaise Pascal

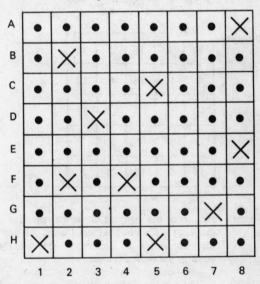

339

8H–6G–4H–2G–1E–2C–1A–3B–5A–7B–
8D–7F
T H E L A S T T H I N G

6H–4G–2H–1F–2D–1B–3A–5B–7A–8C–
7E–8G
O N E D I S C O V E R S

6F–7H–8F–7D–8B–6A–4B–2A–1C–2E–
1G–3H
I N W R I T I N G A B O

5G–6E–7C–5D–6B–4A–3C–1D–3E–5F–
3G–4E
O K I S W H A T T O P U

6D–4C–5E–3F–4D–6C
T F I R S T

A245 (Q257a)

23	6	19	2	15
4	12	25	8	16
10	18	1	14	22
11	24	7	20	3
17	5	13	21	9

A246 (Q264)   He stands the signpost up so that the arm indicating the place he has come from is pointing in
the right direction. The other arms will then
point in the right directions too.

A247 (Q248)   C. The others are identical pairs except that they
have been rotated.

A248 (Q220d)   6729/13458

A249 (Q236a)   Captivate

A250 (Q243)   *Solution 1*   *Solution 2*
                Orange   – Lemon   Orange   – Seville
                Toreador – Seville   Toreador – Matador
                Bull   – Matador   Bull   – Ring
                Diamond – Ring   Diamond – Wedding
                Nuptials – Wedding   Nuptials – Nubile
                Maiden   – Nubile   Maiden   – Horse*
                Sea   – Horse   Sea   – Swordfish
                Sole   – Swordfish   Sole   – Lemon

        * Horses which have not won a race are called maidens.

A251 (Q236e)   Turquoise

A252 (Q222)   The old time is fourteen times the new, so the
               new velocity is fourteen times the old.

$$\frac{v}{v - 1690} = 14$$

               Therefore $v = 1820$ inches per minute.

A253 (Q237b)   Lackadaisically

A254 (Q268)   To solve this problem, treat the avenues and
               streets separately. If everyone lived on the same
               street, the avenues would look like this:

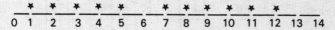

               Number 7, the middle one, would be quickest.
                  If they all lived on the same avenue, then the
               streets would look like this:

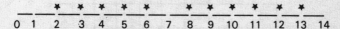

               Number 8, the middle one, would be quickest.
                  Therefore, they would meet on avenue 7,
               street 8.

A255 (Q211) Negligence (Carelessness)
             Ignoble   (Dishonourable)
             Gratitude   (Thankfulness)
             Macabre   (Gruesome)
             Archetype   (Prototype)
             Sample   (Specimen)
             Ignore   (Disregard)
             Genuine   (Authentic)

A256 (Q203) Like so many puzzles of its type this looks much
             more complicated than it really is. In fact, it has a
             beautifully simple solution. The trick is first to
             work out how long it takes the man to walk home.
             You know that the dog has been running for all
             this time at its given constant speed, so it is then a
             simple matter to work out how many miles it has
             covered during this period.

             In this case the man walks for 7 miles at
             3 m.p.h., which means he takes $2\frac{1}{3}$ hours or 2
             hours 20 minutes. The dog is therefore running
             for $2\frac{1}{3}$ hours at 8 m.p.h., which means it covers
             $18\frac{2}{3}$ miles.

A257 (Q259)

92	99	1	8	15	67	74	51	58	40
98	80	7	14	16	73	55	57	64	41
4	81	88	20	22	54	56	63	70	47
85	87	19	21	3	60	62	69	71	28
36	93	25	2	9	61	68	75	52	34
17	24	76	83	90	42	49	26	33	65
23	5	82	89	91	48	30	32	39	66
79	6	13	95	97	29	31	38	45	72
10	12	94	96	78	35	37	44	46	53
11	18	100	77	84	36	43	50	27	59

A258 (Q241) A. Snow goose B. Sidestep C. Harebell D. Jaywalking E. Killer whale F. Plimsoll line G. Deerstalker H. Toffee-nosed I. Tightfisted J. Rubber stamp K. Shorthand L. Space woman

Odd word: Silver

A259 (Q212) Noble   (Illustrious)
             Income   (Revenue)
             Guile   (Cunning)
             Manacle   (Handcuff)
             Avarice   (Covetousness)
             Severe   (Rigorous)
             Immobile   (Motionless)
             Giraffe   (Camelopard)

A260 (Q221) 20–1

Odds	Odds + stake	Divide each one into 100	Staked amount	Any horse to win
2½	3½	=	28.57	100
3½	4½	=	22.22	100
4½	5½	=	18.18	100
5	6	=	16.67	100
10	11	=	9.09	100
16	17	=	5.88	100
20	21	=	4.76	100
20	21	=	4.76	100
			110.13	100

(A bookmaker tries to balance his book – that is, by giving odds lower than true odds and taking money on the horses that he wishes to. He can therefore win, whichever horse wins the race. To assess the position at any given time, he finds out how much he would have to take in order to pay £100 on the winner. If the takings are over £100 he will win; if they are under £100 he will lose.)

A261 (Q245)

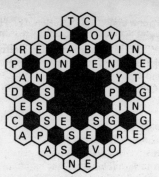

A262 (Q282)   *Across:* Banal, Canard, Hazard, Arab, Dastard, Amass, Lascar
Down: Ananas, Abyss, Adamant, Canal, Walls, Jack, Macaw

L	S	T	B	S	N	W
S	N	R	N	C	J	D
H	S	Z	L	D	R	C
B	Y	D	C	W	K	R
T	B	D	D	L	S	R
N	M	N	S	L	S	M
N	L	M	C	R	C	S

Across answers are ringed
Down answers are not ringed

A263 (Q294)   The two adjacent sides of the rectangle total 23 miles. Hence, if 'm' miles be one side of the rectangle $(m + 4 \times 23 - m + 5) = 2m (23 - m)$, so 'm' is either 14 or 8. The Governor had had in mind a rectangle 15 miles by 8 miles (which is half the area of a rectangle 20 miles by 12 miles). The applicant selected a rectangle 14 miles by 9 miles (which is half the area of a rectangle 18 miles by 14 miles). So the area in question was 126 square miles.

A264 (Q228) 494209

The sequence comprises the squares of successive Kaprekar numbers. A Kaprekar number is one which, when it is squared and when the result is divided into two sets of digits – one to the left and one to the right – produces numbers which can then be added to give the original square root. The first few Kaprekar numbers are: 1, 9, 45, 55, 99, 297, 703, 999, etc. For example:

$$9^2 = 81 \qquad 8 + 1 = 9$$
$$55^2 = 3025 \qquad 30 + 25 = 55$$
$$297^2 = 88209 \qquad 88 + 209 = 297$$
$$703^2 = 494209 \qquad 494 + 209 = 703$$

A265 (Q280) *Across:* Backs, Jog, Dim, Zephyr
Down: Quantify, Slow, Vex

A266 (Q301) Three-letter: FOB – IRE
Four-letter: CROP – FURS
Five-letter: COBRA – FREUD

A267 (Q305) They were all British Prime Ministers: Heath, Home, Eden, Law, Peel, Grey, North.

A268 (Q272) so that when viewed in a mirror the numbers 1, 2, 3, 4, 5 appear in sequence.

A269 (Q204) It is not. Consider all the mothers who have only one child. Half of the children will be boys, half girls. Mothers of the girls will then have a second child. Again there will be an even distribution of boys and girls. Half of these mothers will then go

345

on to have a third child and again there will be as many boys as girls. Regardless of the number of rounds and the size of the families, the sex ratio will obviously always be one to one.

A270 (Q215)   1. Apron – Pinafore 2. Out – Elsewhere 3. Call – Proclaim 4. Send – Transmit 5. Soak – Permeate 6. Sober – Temperate 7. Meek – Gentle 8. Late – Deceased 9. Wit – Badinage 10. Par – Standard 11. Head – Cranium 12. Cup – Trophy 13. Smell – Redolence 14. Lark – Escapade

A271 (Q252b)

×				+	
	○		○		×
		△	△	○	
+	+	△	△	×	
	×			+	
	○				

A272 (Q240)   A. Trappist monk B. Principal boy C. Drill sergeant D. Jury-rigged E. Basking shark F. Spoonbill G. Stonewall H. Freelance I. Roadrunner J. Snapdragon K. Red Admiral L. Filing cabinet
  Odd word: Squash

A273 (Q232)   52631579 × 29 = 1526315791

A274 (Q236d)   Bystander

A275 (Q251)   C. In the outer circle a dot is added at 90° each time. In the middle circle the number of dots increases by one each time and the first dot moves through 90°, with the additional dots placed at 45° intervals. In the inner circle the number of dots increases by one each time and the first dot moves through 45°, with the additional dots placed at 45° intervals.

A276 (Q220a) 3187/25496

A277 (Q257d)

14	3	11	13	24
19	23	7	10	6
20	15	1	17	12
4	22	25	9	5
8	2	21	16	18

A278 (Magic square introduction)

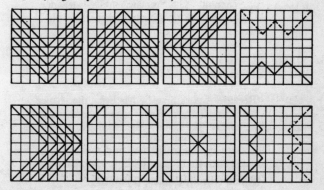

A279 (Q227) 29
When one lot was taken from a total of 89 the remainder was divisible by three. There are only four possibilities:

	A	B	C	D
Total	89	89	89	89
They took	5	14	23	29
Leaving	84	75	66	60
Red	56	50	44	40
Blue	28	25	22	20
Remaining	6	5	5	5
lots	12	6	6	6
	14	12	12	12
	23	23	14	14
	29	29	.29	23

Groups must break into a 2 to 1 ratio. Only D fits:
$$6 + 14 = 20$$
$$5 + 12 + 23 = 40$$

A280 (Q261) It is still a magic square upside down and backwards.

A281 (Q205) Pyx, Myrrh, Why, Sylph, Syzygy, Rhythm, Lymph, Sly, Shyly, Shy, Slyly, Spy, Try, Ply

A282 (Q223) A = 4/7
B = 2/7
C = 1/7
(Because A goes first, he has twice the chance that B has. Because B goes second, he has twice the chance that C has – therefore 4 to 2 to 1.)

A283 (Q206) Thread   The rest are all headless birds: (R)ail, (K)not, (C)row, (F)inch, (P)lover.

A284 (Q258)

5	7	3	8	4
4	1	2	9	2
6	2	5	7	7
4	1	3	6	4
8	7	5	6	1

A285 (Q281)   1. Deciduous 2. Earthworm 3. Hyperbole
4. Magnitude 5. Recumbent 6. Witticism
7. Hidebound 8. Liquorice 9. Loincloth

A286 (Q287)

C	O	N	C	E	R	T
R		I		V		R
A	V	E	R	A	G	E
M		C		D		A
P	R	E	T	E	X	T

A287 (Q300a)

S	P	O	R	T
P	A	P	E	R
O	P	I	N	E
R	E	N	E	W
T	R	E	W	S

S	T	A	F	F
T	I	L	E	R
A	L	A	T	E
F	E	T	E	S
F	R	E	S	H

A288 (Q266) He purchased a suitcase 36 in × 24 in and placed the sword in diagonally.

A289 (Q276–3) 'In general, the art of government consists in taking as much money as possible from one party of the citizens to give to the other.' Voltaire

A290 (Q292) Get out your conversion tables. Convert:

Miles to Centimetres
Acres to Hectares
Litres to Ounces
Tons to Pounds

MALT = CHOP

A291 (Q270) The driver's reasoning was incorrect. If the birds had flown upwards at an accelerated speed the overall weight would have decreased. If the birds had flown downward or fallen in free fall the weight would have increased. As the birds would have flown at random these two effects would have cancelled each other out and the overall weight would have remained the same.

A292 (Q239b) Knickerbockers

A293 (Q217)

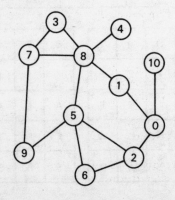

A294 (Q263)

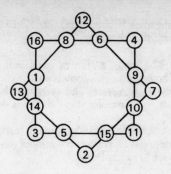

A295 (Q256)   Think
Huff
Oar
Millet
Authority
Shun
Chested
Athos
Ravine
Either
Waggle

Quotation: 'Here lies a king that ruled, as he
thought fit, The universal monarchy of wit.'
Author: Thomas Carew

A296 (Q214a)   Perpendicular

A297 (Q302)

M	inut	E
E	xclamatio	N
N	avigat	E
T	ea	R
A	spirin	G
L	ibert	Y

A298 (Q230)   190 (19 + 18 + 17 + 16 + 15 + 14 + 13 + 12 +
11 + 10 + 9 + 8 + 7 + 6 + 5 + 4 + 3 + 2 + 1)

A299 (Q246)   Kangaroos, Kibbutz, Kinkajou, Kibitzer, Kaolin, Kingfisher, Kettles

A300 (Q210)   1. The eyes 2. Fasten your seat belts 3. Hibernated 4. Switchboard 5. Sahara Desert 6. A merry Christmas and a happy New Year 7. Name for ship 8. Venus de Milo

A301 (Q255)   'Prosperity is not without many fears and distastes; and adversity is not without comforts and hopes.' Francis Bacon

A302 (Q275)   Take the letter immediately after the first vowel in each word to reveal the message: 'Come up and see me some time.'

A303 (Q271)   * = asterisk (ass to risk)

A304   (Kickself (ii) introduction) The whip

A305 (Q202)   They are all anagrams of American States: Maine (A mine), Oklahoma (A holm oak), Utah (A hut).

A306 (Q257e)

15	4	20	16	10
2	19	18	23	3
21	25	1	7	11
5	9	14	13	24
22	8	12	6	17

A307 (Q276–1)'An optimist is a man who starts a crossword puzzle with a fountain pen.'

A308 (Q309)   GI = Gemini W = Water
In each segment of the circle are the first and last

letters of the astrological signs surrounding the initial letter of their corresponding element.

In astrology the word triplicities is another name for the elements: Fire, Earth, Air and Water.

A309 (Q286)   *Across:* Quacks, Brightly, Fez
              Down: Mops, Wavy, Jinxed

A310   (Kickself (ii) introduction) They cannot fall down the hole.

A311 (Q297)

A312 (Q312)   The last fact given means that no one married his son and daughter to the son and daughter of the same friend.

Let us call the five friends by their initials.

'Daughter-in-law of the father of A's son-in-law' means 'A's daughter. 'Son-in-law of the father of C's daughter-in-law' means C's son. Then A's daughter is the sister-in-law of B's son, which can only mean that her brother (A's son) married B's daughter. Similarly, C married his daughter to D's son.

Who is the husband of D's daughter? He cannot be C's or A's son. Let us suppose he is B's son. Then C's daughter's mother-in-law is Mrs

D, while A's son's mother-in-law is Mrs B. So D's daughter can't have married B's son.

It follows that D's daughter married E's son. D's daughter and B's son have a common mother-in-law: Mrs E.

Eugene's daughter is married to Bernard's son.

A313 (Q278)   *Across:* 2. Log 4. Aisle 6. Pensive
8. Boot 9. Belt 11. Darn 12. Need
14. Fort 15. Grip 16. Toil 18. Rasp
19. Noel 21. Dine 22. Nearest
24. Knock 25. Elk

Down: 1. Moss 2. Lint 3. Glib 4. Aeon
5. Even 6. Portion 7. Elegant
8. Baron 10. Terse 11. Dot 13. Dip
17. Leek 18. Risk 20. Lane 21. Deck
23. Roll

A314   (Kickself (ii) introduction)
The coin could not have been marked BC before the birth of Christ.

A315 (Q306)   Peace, Physics, Chemistry (Nobel Prizes)
Amity, Harmony, Concord (Peace)
Douglas, Harrier, Comet (Aeroplanes)
Astronomy, Star, Planet (Astronomy)

A316 (Q279)

A317 (Q250)   A. The three rectangles produce three triangles.

A318 (Q285)

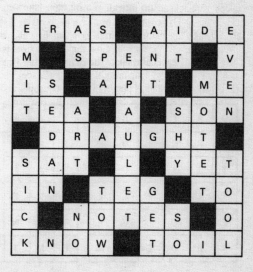

S	L	A	P			S	P	E	W
L	A	P			P			R	O	E
I	M	P	R	U	D	E	N	T
P		E			T	S			S
		T	A	P			A	C	E	
A			L			M			R			B
C	R	I	N	O	L	I	N	E
H	E	N			W			B	I	T
E	D	G	Y			P	E	T	S

A319 (Q213b)   The theme is American presidents: Reagan (age ran), Garfield (gild fear), Harding (rig hand), Madison (maid son), Truman (run mat), Monroe (no more), Washington (showing tan)

A320 (Q225)   117649 (this is a list of cube numbers where either the final digit or the final two digits is their cube root: for example, $51^3 = 132651$)

A321 (Q299)

B	A	T	T	E	R
A	R	R	I	V	E
T	R	I	P	O	D
T	I	P	P	L	E
E	V	O	L	V	E
R	E	D	E	E	M

E	S	T	A	T	E
S	H	A	V	E	N
T	A	L	E	N	T
A	V	E	R	S	E
T	E	N	S	E	R
E	N	T	E	R	S

A322 (Q236b) Juxtapose

A323 (Q310) D. To spell out the word SEMAPHORE in semaphore.

A324 (Q252a)

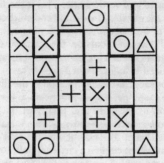

A325 (Q235) 1. Dock 2. Hope 3. Salary 4. Haze
5. Guitar 6. Jaw 7. Qualm 8. Box
9. Fauna 10. Dove

A326 (Kickself (ii) introduction) 1989 × 50p = £994.50;
1988 ×.50p = £994.00

A327 (Q218) 37½ m.p.h.
If the distance to be covered is, say, 60 miles and the car is travelling at 50 m.p.h., the journey will take 1 hour 12 minutes. At 30 m.p.h. the same journey will take 2 hours. This means that it takes 3 hours 12 minutes to cover 120 miles or 1 hour to cover 37½ miles.

A328 (Q249) G.

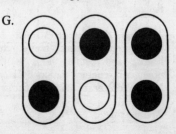

There are two separate elements in this puzzle. Taking the black and white circles inside the enclosure, there are three different possible combinations, as indicated on p. 134, and one each of these combinations appears on each horizontal and vertical line. This is the first element of the puzzle. The second and more complex part is to work out what is happening with the 'X' and 'O' symbols outside the enclosure. The last square in each horizontal and vertical line is produced as follows: when two circles or two crosses appear in the same position in the first two parts of each line, a symbol appears in the same position in the third and final part but is changed from a circle to a cross, or vice versa. For example, looking along line one the first and second parts both contain a circle top left, so in the third part a symbol appears in the same position, but is a cross. In the same line a cross appears in the first and second parts top right, so in the third part a symbol appears in the same position, but is a circle. This procedure is repeated in each horizontal and vertical line.

A329   (Magic Square introduction)

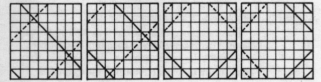

A330 (Q236c) Kingsized

A331 (Q234)   They have all different, established and accepted spellings in America: honor, check, theater, license and center. This is the result of nineteenth-century nationalism on the part of Noah Webster, of *Webster's Dictionary* fame.

A332 (Q214c) Architecture

A333 (Q233)   A, AT, ATE, RATE, TREAT, RATTLE, STARLET (STARTLE), SLATTERN, TRANSLATE

Variations may be possible on the smaller words.

A334 (Q283)   *Across:* Referee (in charge of a football match), Dropped (fallen out), Noisier (sounds louder), Sisters (twin girls)
Down: Rodents (mice), Florins (silver pieces), Reptile (snake), Endures (puts up with)

A335 (Q300b)

S	H	A	F	T
H	U	L	L	O
A	L	L	A	Y
F	L	A	K	E
T	O	Y	E	D

A336 (Q304)   The names are all anagrams:

Zena le Vue	= Venezuela (the Americas)
Dr A. Glebe	= Belgrade (Europe)
Rob E. Lumen	= Melbourne (Australasia)
Ann Ziata	= Tanzania (Africa)

A337 (Q308)   In the **cove** near **hove** **rafters** tend to **rake** and **span** and **slot** home on **buildings**.

In the same **cove** your **outer** **charm** will be the **downfall** of a **gang** of **husky** **gamblers**.

You can **hear** the **snide** remarks of a **wisp** of **blushing** **kennel** maids as they **drift** and **clamour** and **mingle** and **hover** and **cry** at the **observance** of a **dray** full of **troops**.

Coven of Witches   Gam of Whales
Hover of Crows   Earth of Foxes
Rafter of Turkeys   Nide of Pheasant
Erst of Bees   Wisp of Snipe
Rake of Colts   Blush of Boys
Span of Mules   Kennel of Raches
Sloth of Bears   Drift of Wild Pigs
Building of Rooks   Clamour of Rooks
Covey of Partridge   Glean of Herrings
Rout of Wolves   Hover of Crows
Charm of Finches   Cry of Hounds
Down of Sheep   Observance of Hermits
Fall of Woodcock   Rayful of Knaves
Gang of Elk   Troop of Foxes
Husk of Hares

A338 (Q239a)   Misapprehension

A339 (Q219) $((1\cdot5 + 0\cdot25) \times \dfrac{60}{50})$

= 2·1 mins or 2 minutes 6 seconds

A340 (Q220c)   2943/17658

A341 (Q257c)

25	10	3	6	21
22	12	19	8	4
11	9	13	17	15
2	18	7	14	24
5	16	23	20	1

A342 (Q229)   58 inches
       The ordinary schoolboy would rightly treat
this as a quadratic equation. Here is the actual
arithmetic.
       Double the product of the two distances from
the walls. This gives us 144, which is the square

of 12. The sum of the two distances is 17. If we add these two numbers, 12 and 17, together and also subtract one from the other, we get the two answers: either 29 or 5 was the radius, which means that the diameter was 58 inches or 10 inches. A table of the latter dimensions would be absurd, so the former must be correct.

A343 (Q244)   Enrage, Geisha, Haggle, Legato, Topple, Legion, Onrush, Shaken

A344 (Q267)   79 years (there was not a year 0)

A345 (Q289)

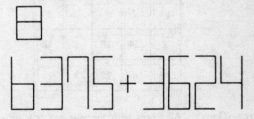

The sum consists of the *unused* segments when displaying the numbers of a seven-segment LED display: that is,

A346 (Q277)   This is a straight substitution cryptogram where each letter of the alphabet is represented by its own symbol. Decoded the quotation reads: 'The least thing upset him on the links. He missed short putts because of the uproar of butterflies in the adjoining meadow.' P. G. Wodehouse

A347 (Q201)   Bed. All words can be prefixed with Hot.

A348 (Q298)

R	U	D	E	R
U	V	U	L	A
D	U	C	A	T
E	L	A	T	E
R	A	T	E	D

S	O	L	I	D
O	P	E	R	A
L	E	G	A	L
I	R	A	T	E
D	A	L	E	S

A349 (Q273)   40. There must have been an even number of
men to receive the answers given.

A350 (Q214b)   Reservation

A351 (Q257b)

17	5	10	20	13
16	23	14	8	4
11	7	1	25	21
2	24	18	9	12
19	6	22	3	15

A352 (Q207)   All begin with the number one in a different
language:
        (En)umerate – Danish
        (Uno)ccupied – Italian and Spanish
        (One)rous – English
        (Un)usual – French
        (Bir)d – Turkish

A353 (Q216)   Pomfret, Herring, Lamprey, Halibut
Key anagram: Grouper

A354 (Q290)

3	×	12	÷	3	=	12
+		+		+		×
9	+	15	÷	3	=	8
÷		÷		−		÷
3	+	9	÷	2	=	6
=		=		=		=
4	×	3	+	4	=	16

A355 (Q242)   1. Cast 2. Song 3. Rest 4. Foot 5. Over
6. Word 7. Hill 8. Wind 9. Rush 10. Face

A356 (Q237a) Notwithstanding

A357 (Q254)   I, It, Fit, Wend, Motet, Tattoo, Shunned, Lethargy, Casserole

A358 (Q213a) The theme is mammals: Beaver (rave be), Porcupine (upper coin), Whale (he law), Dolphin (hold pin), Anteater (neat rate), Leopard (role pad), Muskrat (rum task)

A359 (Q293)   The Law of the Search: 'The first place to look for anything is the last place you would expect it to be.'

A360 (Q296)   *Across:* Jamb, Chintzy, Elk, Fops
Down: Waxy, Quivers, Dog

A361 (Q260)

13	8	12	1
2	11	7	14
3	10	6	15
16	5	9	4

A362 (Q288) Yes, in 166 seconds
  54 seconds = 0·9 minutes, reciprocal* = 1·11
  48 seconds = 0·8 minutes, reciprocal = 1·25
                                    add 2·36
  30 seconds = 0·5 minutes, reciprocal = 2·00

  Reciprocal = 2·777 minutes   deduct 0.36
            =   166 seconds

  * In mathematics, a reciprocal is a number or quantity
  which, when multiplied by a given number or quantity,
  gives the product of 1, that is, 0·8 × 1·25 = 1. To find
  the reciprocal of 0·8, it is necessary to divide 1 by 0·8,
  which gives the reciprocal 1·25.

A363 (Q311) Len. The letters of his name are contained in his
  relationship to me, uncle, as was the case with the
  other relatives mentioned.

A364   (Kickself (ii) introduction) They were triplets, and
  the third one was a girl.

A365 (Q209) **CACOPHONY**

O	P	C	N	C	P
C	Y	H	O	Y	O
C	P	A	C	O	N
H	N	O	C	A	H
A	Y	P	H	Y	O
O	C	A	N	O	C

A366 (Q274)   Total up each group of three numbers and take the corresponding letter of the alphabet. Decoded the message reads: 'The paradox is a cunning beast.'

A367 (Q307)   In both cases only two.

A368 (Q284)   *Across:* Careers, Natives, Forgone, Resists
              Down: Conifer, Retires, Envious, Systems

A369 (Q295) $7^3 - 6^3 - 3^3 = 100$
              $1870^3 - 1797^3 - 903^3 = 100$

A370 (Q269)   As water is slightly heavier than wine, if you remove the bung, remove the bottle cap, upend the full bottle of water over the bung hole and make a good seal, the water will be exchanged for wine.

A371 (Q247)   B. Each shape moves round once clockwise at each stage. The dot moves two positions. Once the dot has landed in a particular shape, that shape then changes to a new shape in the next diagram.

A372 (Q276–2) 'The man who smiles when things go wrong has thought of someone he can blame it on.' Jones' Law

A373 (Q303)   24 minutes.
              There are two simple formulas for working out the answer to this puzzle.
              (a) Total time difference, 30 minutes, less time saved, 12 minutes – that is, 18 minutes – plus one half time saved – that is, 6 minutes = 24 minutes.
              (b) Subtract one half time saved, 6 minutes, from total time difference, 30 minutes = 24 minutes.
              If you do not know either of the formulas, the answer can be worked out by logic. As I leave according to my usual schedule, we know it is

before 5.30 p.m. when I pick up my wife. Because we have saved 12 minutes, that must be the same time that it takes me to drive from the point I picked her up, to the station, and back to that same point. Assuming it takes an equal 6 minutes each way I have therefore picked up my wife 6 minutes before I would normally do so, which means 5.24 p.m. So my wife must have walked from 5 p.m. to 5.24 p.m. or for 24 minutes.

A374 (Q291)

Paint			Possible ways
Red	Blue	Faces	of painting
12	0		2
11	1		2
10	2		6
9	3		10
8	4		24
7	5		28
6	6		24
			96

A375 (Q238) Categorise, Feathered, Woebegone, Together, Attendance, Fatherless, Inhabitant, Malefactor, Redevelop, Damageable

A376 (Q226) *Across:* 4489, 1225, 4761, 2809, 3969, 5329, 4225, 3136
Down: 2916, 1156, 6561, 7921, 4624, 5929, 9604, 3249

A377 (Q262)

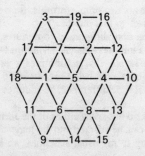

A378   (Kickself (ii) introduction) No doors are shown, so
         they must be on the opposite side. This would
         then be the kerb side. In Britain the bus would
         therefore be travelling towards 'B'.

A379 (Q265)   It contains the numbers 1 to 9 in alphabetical
                order.

A380   (More Anagrams introduction) Bayonet

A381   (More Numbers introduction) 381654729

A382   (Word Play introduction) 1. Cleave
         2. Sequoia   3. Triennially (Tinily and Renal)
         4. Nominates (Minnesota)   5. Manufacture
         (also, of course, Manufactured, Manufacturer/s,
         Manufacturing)   6. Queueing   7. Best,
         Worst